The Hour That Matters Most

the Hour that Matters Most

THE SURPRISING POWER OF THE FAMILY MEAL

LES & LESLIE PARROTT
WITH STEPHANIE ALLEN
TINA KUNA

Tyndale House Publishers, Inc.

CAROL STREAM, ILLINOIS

Visit Tyndale online at www.tyndale.com.

Visit Les and Leslie's website at www.realrelationships.com.

Visit the Dream Dinners website at www.dreamdinners.com.

TYNDALE and Tyndale's quill logo are registered trademarks of Tyndale House Publishers, Inc.

The Hour That Matters Most: The Surprising Power of the Family Meal

Designed by Ron Kaufmann

Published in association with Yates & Yates (www.yates2.com).

Library of Congress Cataloging-in-Publication Data

Parrott, Les.
    The hour that matters most : the surprising power of the family meal / Les and Leslie Parrott with Stephanie Allen and Tina Kuna.
        p. cm.
    Includes bibliographical references (p.   ).
    ISBN 978-1-4143-3744-9 (sc)
1. Families—Religious life. 2. Communication in families—Religious aspects—Christianity. 3. Dinners and dining—Religious aspects—Christianity. 4. Cooking—Religious aspects—Christianity. I. Parrott, Leslie. II. Title.
    BV4526.3.P36 2011
    249—dc23   2011021931

Printed in the United States of America

17   16   15   14   13   12   11
7   6   5   4   3   2   1

Contents

Other things may change us,

but we start and end with family.

ANTHONY BRANDT

A Note from Tina and Stephanie:

Just as we were going to press with this book, we received some news that none of us expected. News that all of us dread to some extent. Especially if you're a woman. If you're a man, you worry about it striking your wife, sister, or daughter. Breast cancer. Within just weeks of wrapping up this project, Tina was diagnosed with an aggressive form of breast cancer. It's an early-stage diagnosis, thanks to a routine mammogram, but it will require an aggressive treatment in response. Strong and unshaken in her passion to change America, Tina has found that this diagnosis only further galvanizes her reasons for writing this book: to strengthen America from its core—the family.

In this strained economy, at a time when many dual-income families are struggling just to get by, the idea of a 1950's-style, sit-down-at-the-dinner-table meal might seem impossible. Too idealistic. Too unrealistic.

But that's not our message, and we haven't written a book to make you feel guilty. That's the last thing you need. Studies show that 65 percent of teens and young adults spend less than an hour a day unplugged. And that is exactly our call.

Stop.

Unplug.

Postpone that text or conference call.

Have dinner together (or any meal, for that matter). Because as Tina's recent diagnosis reminds us, you never know when your life is going to change. Something might happen that reminds you that the only thing that really matters is your family.

We believe that your dinner hour is truly the hour that matters most. And we need to fight for it.

Introduction

Once upon a Mealtime

*Along with getting enough exercise, making your own
meals from healthy ingredients is one of the most
important things you can do to stay fit and healthy. And
sharing those meals at sit-down family dinners models
this healthy behavior to your children. They'll carry that
valuable nutrition lesson with them for life.*

BOB GREENE

I WAS SORTING through old childhood photographs with
my husband, Les, when we discovered a long-lost Polaroid
taken on my seventh birthday. Though I was sporting a
giant smile in my purple paisley birthday outfit, the main
character of the photograph was not me, but the cake. For
some reason my mom had invited me to decorate my own
birthday cake that year, and with a burst of creative energy
and flourish, I had arranged everything imaginable on that
cake, from porcelain figurines (overwhelmingly large for
the cake) to colorful birthday cards pushed right into the
frosting, which held them firmly upright. The frosting had
become my celebration canvas, and I relished it.

When my husband saw the photo he immediately

commented, "If there is a snapshot that captures your spirit, this is the one." I love celebrations with my family, and I especially take great pleasure from a chance to be creative with food on special occasions—or even just the more mundane moments of life that need to be remembered.

This is exactly what was weighing on my mind and even aching in my soul as I rushed to get our two little boys set up for dinner at the kitchen island—rather than do what I really wanted, have the whole family sit down at our kitchen table. This mealtime, like so many others, was not sitting right with me.

In fact, as I was preparing what each boy liked (with help from some prepackaged food ready to microwave)— chicken nuggets, fruit, and yogurt for Jackson; mac and cheese, carrots, and yogurt for John—I realized that this was never the picture I had in mind for our family routine. Once I served the boys, I started the risotto simmering on the stove that Les had requested for his dinner while I rummaged through the fridge for random veggies to toss into an oversize salad for me. The boys were already off their counter stools and back to the playroom before Les carried his dish to sit in front of the television to watch the news. Thus concluded another typical "family dinner hour" at our home.

How could it be? This is never what I wanted. My kitchen had turned into a food court and my family members were customers. I always dreamed that we'd have a shared meal together on most nights, just as I did as a kid growing up in my family. I imagined that dinner would be the backdrop to lively conversations and lots of laughter with my husband and our boys. I envisioned setting the table with a bit of creative flair on occasion, like minichalkboard place cards, or "search and find" place mats, and maybe a cake decorated in a surprising way from time to time!

But somewhere in the fray of raising our busy boys and managing fast-paced schedules and catering to different taste buds, I lost sight of that vision for dinner. Or maybe I was simply letting it go. Reluctantly. Almost unconsciously. After all, I still had the vision and wanted it realized—that's why I still felt a pang of guilt and an uneasiness in my spirit each night. At first, I'd say to myself, *I'll get us all around the table for a common meal tomorrow.* But that "tomorrow" kept getting put off. My dream of a happy and healthy family dinner hour was becoming a distant memory. It had all but dried up—until I met Stephanie Allen and Tina Kuna.

You'll meet them, too, in the following chapter. But before we get to Stephanie and Tina, Les and I thought it might be helpful to give you a quick picture of why so many of us have left our mothers' kitchens and why the common family meal too often seems like a forgotten fairy tale.

THE DECADE THAT CHANGED OUR DINNERS

"Can I take your order please?" The voice comes from a small scratchy speaker just outside the driver's side window. You tell the lighted menu board what you want and then you "pull around to the pickup window" where your food, wrapped in colored paper and cardboard, is ready to go in a paper bag. Lickety-split.

Before fast food ruled the world, people used to sit around the dinner table, leisurely eating home-cooked meals and enjoying good discussions, laughter, debate, and uninterrupted conversation. After all, there weren't many options. But that all changed beginning in the 1950s when a few self-made men in Southern California defied conventional opinion and began setting up stands where people could buy food on the go. From their cars. Fast. It wasn't long before the fast-food industry transformed not only our diet but our landscape, economy, workforce, and culture.

Today, the McDonald's Corporation is the nation's largest purchaser of beef, pork, and potatoes. It spends more money on advertising and marketing than any other brand. As Eric Schlosser, author of the disturbing *Fast Food Nation*, writes, "The impact of McDonald's on the way we live today is hard to overstate. The Golden Arches are now more widely recognized than the Christian cross." And McDonald's is just one of the hundreds of companies that make up the fast-food industry.

Fast food's impact on families enjoying a slow-paced, home-cooked meal around the dinner table almost goes without saying. In America over the past twenty-five years, dinners at home have dropped 33 percent.[1] In just one generation, at least a third of us have all but lost the meaning of a meal in which the family shares the experience.

Dinnertime is no longer expected. Meals have become fast-food pit stops to keep us going as we move from one activity to another. We often eat solo while doing something else, such as working, driving, reading, or surfing online. And even when we eat at home, it's often a nutritionally questionable, heat-and-eat meal substitute from the supermarket that's nuked in the microwave.

DID YOU KNOW?
Over the last few decades, fast food has infiltrated every nook and cranny of American society. In 1970, Americans spent about $6 billion on fast food; today they spend more than $110 billion. Americans now spend more on fast food than on movies, books, magazines, newspapers, videos, and recorded music—combined.

GOBBLE-GULP-AND-GO IS NO WAY TO LIVE
About the same time the drive-through was being born in Southern California, Swanson unveiled the first TV dinner—a highly processed, all-in-one platter containing turkey with cornbread dressing and gravy, sweet potatoes, and buttered peas. And not long after that, another culinary time-saver made its debut: instant rice. Uncle Ben got in on the idea by promising housewives "Long grain rice that's ready in . . . five minutes!"

In the 1970s, cooking at home moved from being measured in minutes to being timed in seconds. With the introduction of the microwave oven, the original Swanson's TV dinner that took twenty-five minutes to cook in a conventional oven now seemed painfully slow.

Somewhere in the mid 1950s, food became less about its flavor and nutritional value and more about how little time it took to be ready to eat. Cooking, it was decided, was a chore that didn't deserve our time. And in the rush to speed through the kitchen or bypass it altogether, the intrinsic relational value of a home-cooked meal was unwittingly lost. The humble ritual of hanging out in the kitchen on a regular basis with family members was pushed aside, never recognized for how critically important it is for strengthening family ties and giving kids an unparalleled advantage.

THERE'S A BETTER WAY—AND IT'S EASIER THAN YOU THINK

When you allow the fast-food mentality to infiltrate the majority of your meals, you are missing out on one of the very best means of building the kind of family you long for. Why? Because a meal prepared at home, where the family gathers around a table, nourishes the core of who we are and who our children become.

Think about it. What happens in your family when you collectively step off the treadmill to actually sit down without a scheduled appointment nipping at your heels or a smartphone begging for attention? A meal where you don't hear or say things like, "We've got to order fast" or "We don't have time for dessert" or "We've got to eat quickly." Maybe, like so many, you can't remember the last time you enjoyed slowly eating food together. Maybe you've missed out on the magical rewards of this modest mealtime. Or maybe you haven't learned to leverage it for all it's worth.

No matter—this book is devoted to helping you reclaim your family dinnertime and reap the surprising rewards it has to offer. And it's easier than you think. No guilt required. In dozens of practical ways, we're going to show you how. The chapters that follow are little treasure troves of information to help you. Each chapter includes a stand-alone recipe you can whip up with little effort. We're not going to bog you down with weighty chapters to make a case you already believe in. We're jumping straight into the practice of enjoying family meals, which until now, you may have only imagined. And we're confident you will see the benefits of this practice around your own table.

WHY WE WROTE THIS BOOK

As a psychologist (Les) and a marriage and family therapist (Leslie) who specialize in relationships, we have devoted our professional lives to finding out what works and what doesn't when it comes to building healthy connections. It's our business to know what research is showing us about what strategies truly make a difference. And in our research we keep running into the same surprising and unavoidable fact: families that share a dinnertime ritual together—regardless of their stage, class, or race—enjoy innumerable benefits.

When we got out of our rut and found our groove of a routine family meal together, life got easier. It may not seem possible, but it did. Each member of our family has benefited, and the benefits, techniques, and strategies we were implementing around our own dinner table were just too powerful not to share with other parents like you. Truth be told, however, it wasn't until we met Stephanie Allen and Tina Kuna, with their ingenious ideas for maximizing time around the dinner table, that our method began to take shape. Stephanie and Tina, as you are about to see in the first chapter, have their finger on the pulse of family dinnertime like nobody else in the country, and their story is one we're eager to share.

When the four of us began comparing notes, the energy became palpable and we felt more than a mere desire to get this message out. It became a collective calling.

OUR PROMISE TO YOU

We have written every word of this book with you in mind. And we'll be up front about some assumptions we're making. We assume, for example, that you are extremely busy and you don't need anything on your to-do list that doesn't have a significant payoff. In fact, we assume you're looking for ways to recoup more time—quality time—in your home. We also assume you don't need more guilt. We connect with enough household managers to know that you're likely weighed down with things you wish you were already doing but can't seem to pull off when it comes to your kids.

Our biggest assumption about you is that you'd do most anything to make your home a comforting refuge for your family. You want a home that is anchored in connection, buoyed by support, and filled with laughter. In short, you want your family to thrive.

With this in mind, we promise to give you practical and proven tools for making this happen. We will give you sensible takeaways in each chapter of this book. No platitudes. No banal advice. And no shame. Just tried-and-true methods for busy households that are building strong families.

Les and Leslie Parrott

1 | Creating the Safest Place on Earth

Home is an invention on which
no one has yet improved.

ANN DOUGLAS

FROM STEPHANIE

It was a typical November day in the Pacific Northwest: gray and damp outside, and cozy inside. My daughter, Karlene, was home for the first time since leaving for college. We drove up to Anacortes, Washington, on Fidalgo Island, the largest of the San Juan Islands, where my parents live. Along the way we picked up Karlene's "grammy," my mom's mom.

There we were, four generations together, in the kitchen making dinner. With a tea towel over my shoulder and the palms of my hands covered in flour from rolling the dough that would soon become flaky biscuits, I peered into the living room to spy Dad building a crackling fire in the fireplace.

As we gathered around the table that evening, all seemed right with the world. I was home—the safest place on earth. And I realized this feeling is what family is all about.

■ ■ ■

When you're home, you want to breathe deeply, lower your shoulders, and relax. There's a feeling of belonging, acceptance, and contentment. At least there should be. Healthy homes—homes that function as they should—refresh, recharge, and renew. They become places where children's identities find flight and values take root.

For Stephanie Allen, her own home was none of these things. As a busy working mom of two active kids, it was all Stephanie could do to keep up with the demands of the daily schedule. Church youth group, soccer practice, and school activities meant lots of time in the car, and very little time for real interaction among family members.

Stephanie longed for the kinds of relationships she remembered with her own parents and sibling when she was growing up: relationships built on conversation and connection—often forged around the dinner table. She remembered the way her family would linger after a meal just to talk and catch up, and she wished her own family could do the same. But after a long day at work and a couple of hours shuttling kids from one activity to the next, who had time for making elaborate meals? Some days it was all she could do to keep up with everything *and* get a meal on the table for her family. She realized that she needed a game plan.

Stephanie started meeting with a friend once a month to assemble meals for their families. "It was a great time for us to talk and laugh," Stephanie remembers. "And at the end of the day, we each had a month's worth of meals in our freezers, ready to pull out when we needed them. One less thing to stress about." Those monthly "assembly days" provided a sense of liberation from the dreaded daily chore of scrambling home after work to pull together a wholesome dinner for the family.

This practice continued for seven years, and before long, other friends were asking for tips to help them do the same. In 2002, Stephanie decided to host a "monthly meal-prep night" with a group of friends. The response was overwhelming, and it didn't take long for Stephanie to see that she wasn't alone in her desire to share home-cooked meals with her family. After that first night, friends started talking to friends, and e-mail requests for more events started pouring in.

"So many moms are working hard and trying to keep up, but it's really difficult," she says. "The bottom line is that we just want to raise great kids." As it was turning out, the practical solution to getting a regular meal on the dinner table was helping Stephanie and her friends to do just that. "Suddenly, we were having conversations with our kids like never before. They were opening up and lingering around the table. The dinner hour was quickly becoming the hub of our home." And Stephanie was hearing similar stories of building stronger family connections from the other women in the group too.

Without knowing it, Stephanie and her band of "sisters"

had stumbled onto the power of an age-old practice that
has been slowly slipping into extinction. Like so many

> # Food is the most primitive form of comfort.
>
> SHEILA GRAHAM

other women in twenty-first-century
families, Stephanie had all but given
up on having a regular dinnertime
with her family before she tried her
assemble-and-freeze method. But getting a meal on the table without undue
stress wasn't the biggest discovery. No,
Stephanie and her friends had tapped
into a power that gets to the heart of
a healthy home—a power that creates
the safest place on earth.

CREATING COMFORT

Chicken noodle soup, meat loaf, fried chicken, macaroni
and cheese, mashed potatoes and gravy, bread pudding,
brownies, doughnuts, apple pie. These are commonly
referred to as "comfort food," and with good reason. Most
of us find great comfort in a tasty meal we've grown up
with, a meal that doesn't have to be explained by *Gourmet*
or *Saveur* magazines.

But true comfort, the kind that heals emotional hurts
and turns around bad days, involves far more than our
palates. One dictionary defines the word *comfort* as "a
feeling of relief or encouragement," or "contented well-
being."[1] A quick review of the word's origin, though,
uncovers a deeper meaning. We get the verb *to comfort*
from the Latin *com-* + *fortis*, meaning "to make strong"
(that is, like a fortress).

So to comfort literally means to make someone stronger. And that's exactly what you do for your children. Comfort fortifies their spirits. Whenever you encourage your children with uplifting words, console them with a tender touch, relieve their sorrow with your mere presence, support them with heartfelt praise, or provide a wholesome meal and the love that's served with it, you are helping to make your children strong.

WHAT WOULD STRENGTHEN YOUR HOME?

If you could press a magic button to instantly strengthen your home, what would it do? We don't mean the physical house. We mean the feeling, the chemistry, and the climate of the relationships within it. We're talking about the spirit of your home.

Would you want it to include more laughter? Meaningful and engaging conversations? Vulnerability and respect? Mutual support? These are the things most parents mention. And if you're like the hundreds of parents we've surveyed, you're likely to sum up the desire you have for your home by saying you want it to be the safest place on earth.

THE SECRETS OF A HEALTHY HOME

Thriving families don't just happen. Merely going with the flow or taking what comes is fatal to the heart of a home. Healthy and happy families are the result of deliberate intention, determination, and practice. Every family expert will tell you that a healthy home is the result of a proactive parent.

The largest study ever done on family life was con-
ceived on Interstate 40 where it runs through the rolling
hills of Oklahoma and the prairies of western Texas. That's
where University of Alabama professor Nick Stinnett was
driving with his wife, Nancy, when, in the midst of their
discussion on families, he determined to find out what
healthy homes were doing right. Up to that point, family
researchers were focused exclusively on dysfunctional and
fragmenting families. Dr. Stinnett wanted to take a different approach. He wanted to know how people in healthy
homes handled conflict and power struggles. He wanted
to know how they communicated, and so on. In short, he
wanted to know the secrets of healthy families.

That was in 1974, and his study took more than twenty-
five years and involved more than fourteen thousand
families who were ethnically diverse, had many kinds of
religious beliefs, and came from all fifty states and twenty-
four countries around the world. The one thing these families had in common was a thriving, successful, and strong
family unit.

What did the world's largest, longest, and most comprehensive study on family life teach us? First, that
thriving families are not immune to trouble. They suffer
financial setbacks, chronic illnesses, and all the rest. But
in spite of the strain and stress of daily life, they create
pleasant, positive places to live where family members
can count on one another for support, love, and loyalty.
They unite to meet challenges and solve problems. They
pull together. They feel good about themselves as a family and have a deep sense of belonging with each other, a

sense of "*we-ness.*" At the same time, they encourage each person's uniqueness and potential.

In practical terms, the study found that thriving families share six qualities. These are the "secrets" of creating the safest place on earth:

1. **Commitment:** Members of strong families are dedicated to promoting one another's welfare and happiness. They prize their family and value the relationships.
2. **Appreciation and Affection:** Members of strong families are thankful for each other. They don't take their special relationships with one another for granted.
3. **Positive Communication:** Members of strong families spend a lot of time talking freely with one another, doing their best to be understood and to understand.
4. **Time Together:** Members of strong families spend generous amounts of time with one another— quality time—creating memories and building bonds.
5. **Spiritual Well-Being:** Strong families, whether they attend formal religious services or not, have a sense of a greater good that gives them strength and purpose as a unit.
6. **The Ability to Cope with Stress and Crises:** Members of strong families are not fragmented by tension and trouble. They use those experiences to learn and grow together.[2]

There you have it. Six qualities that healthy homes and thriving families all have in common. Look back over the list. Those qualities seem profoundly simple, don't they? But that can be misleading because the fact is, *understanding* what makes a healthy home is not the same as building one. That requires being proactive. And in the pressure cooker of our busy daily lives, being proactive is where most of us get bogged down. When emotions are frazzled, bills are mounting, and time is in short supply, doing something proactive can be the last thing on our minds.

But what if that *doing* were actually easier than you imagined? What if it took less time and were simpler than you could even believe?

That's where *the hour that matters most* comes in. Countless studies have shown that if parents could take only one proactive and practical step to engender family commitment, appreciation, affection, positive communication, time together, and all the rest, it would be to establish a regular dinnertime around a common table without distraction. One hour a few times a week. That's it.

KEEPING THE LIGHT ON

Have you ever given your children "the blessing"? Blessing someone says that you love and accept that person unconditionally. And that's exactly what you give your children when you tune in to their world over a family dinner or any other time. Similar to building them a campfire on a dark night, you draw them toward the warmth of genuine concern and love. And because of it, they'll be drawn to you years down the road.

TWO WAYS TO KEEP THE LIGHTS ON

Keeping the lights on when an older child is out for the evening sends a message that you care about your child, that you are waiting for him or her to return, and that your home is a welcoming and safe place. In the same way, a healthy home "leaves the lights on" by providing a safe place for the family to speak honestly and express their feelings without fear of condemnation. There are two ways a parent can keep the emotional lights on. Let's look at them briefly.

1. Stay Cool

Let's say your seven-year-old blurts out a few shocking words. Or your teenager starts talking about getting a tattoo. Or your twelve-year-old tells you of a plan to stay overnight with a friend you disapprove of. Whatever your child's shocking statement is, your job is to play it cool. Muster your inner strength, stay calm, and give yourself some time by saying something like "That's interesting" or "Tell me more about that." You may be cringing inside, but do your best not to show it. Giving yourself time helps to keep the situation from becoming a major argument or escalating into a shouting match.

The idea is to create a safe place—a place where your child feels free to say whatever is on his or her mind. You can probe, clarify, and explore, but the moment you pass judgment without listening is the moment your child begins to clam up. Of course, this doesn't mean you don't set rules and boundaries. It just means you let your child be heard before you lay down the law. It keeps tears and tantrums to a minimum and, in the process, earns your child's respect.

2. Keep a Confidence

What happens at the dinner table stays at the table—or in the car or wherever you have heart-to-heart conversations with your children. You may think that only adults prize the confidence of others, but it holds true for kids, too. All that needs to happen is for them to hear you talking about them to a friend, saying something that may seem harmless to you but is embarrassing to your children, and you have instantly lost trustworthiness in your kids' eyes.

> The light is what guides you home, the warmth is what keeps you there.
>
> ELLIE RODRIGUEZ

Let's say your son tells you about feeling lonely on the playground or inadequate in art class. You're talking to your girlfriend about whatever comes to mind and you mention your son's name. He pricks up his ears even though he's on the other side of the room watching television. You don't give it a second thought as you tell your girlfriend how your heart is breaking for him during school recess. Your son immediately turns off the tube, goes to his room, and closes the door. *What just happened?* you wonder. He might tell you at some point. Then again, he might not. He may just decide then and there not to talk to you about his feelings again. Like everyone else, he wants to know that his confessions are held in confidence. If they're not, home doesn't feel so safe anymore.

Did You Know?
The majority of teens in America—67 percent— want to spend more time with their parents.

MORE THAN JUST A WHOLESOME MEAL

Without knowing it, Stephanie and her band of "sisters" had stumbled onto the power of an age-old practice that has been slowly slipping into extinction. Before trying her fix-and-freeze method, Stephanie, like so many other women in twenty-first-century families, had all but given up on having a regular family dinnertime. Darting in and out of fast-food joints between work, school plays, and soccer practices, Stephanie didn't realize that she was forfeiting more than just a wholesome meal. However, as she began practicing the fix-and-freeze method, it dawned on her that she was beginning to gain the most treasured sixty minutes of her day.

Late one night, after a group of moms had gone, Stephanie and longtime friend Tina Kuna were up to their elbows in soapsuds. They began talking about the positive difference their little system was proving to make and wondering where it might go. After all, neither felt right turning anyone away. Yet they were getting more requests than they could handle. As it turned out, what began as an attempt to draw their own families together around the table eventually led to a partnership with each other and the founding of a business they call Dream Dinners, a fix-and-freeze company reaching more than one million families each year.

THE DREAM OF DREAM DINNERS

Dream Dinners was founded with a mission of bringing families together around the dinner table. Food and families are at the heart of everything Dream Dinners does as they provide guests who visit their locations with all the ingredients they need for a great meal. Dream Dinners offers freedom from the hassles surrounding the planning and preparation of meals night after night and allows families to come together at the end of the day to eat a delicious, healthy meal. Little could Stephanie and Tina have known just how powerful that one hour around the table would be—both for their own families and for so many others.

In fact, the surprising benefits of this simple ritual are so astounding that even experts on the family are stunned by the findings of recent research. Why? Because the evidence is on the table: if you want a healthy home, a family that gives your children every advantage, and a place where lasting memories are made and feelings of comfort are a given, you can't afford to neglect the hour that matters most.

FROM STEPHANIE

Macaroni and cheese is true comfort food. My son Mitchel loved it (from the blue box). When he was six, I taught him how to make it himself. It was the first really independent thing he could do, and he had a real sense of accomplishment when he made it by himself and ate it for lunch. Sometimes he would ask to make it for friends who were playing at our house. One of my treasured memories is secretly watching him show his friends how to "make" mac and cheese and then serve it with such pride. One year for his birthday dinner he asked if I would make mac and cheese for his party. I got out my cookbooks and created a wonderful, homemade macaroni and cheese in honor of the occasion. What a mistake! When I served it, he cried, "That's not real mac and cheese!" We still laugh about that every time we make Mama's Macaroni and Cheese.

Mama's Macaroni and Cheese (serves 6)

5 cups cooked elbow macaroni (about 1 pound dry)
3 tablespoons butter
2 tablespoons flour
1 teaspoon kosher salt
2 cups 2% milk
1 cup cubed American cheese
1 cup shredded cheddar cheese
1 cup seasoned bread crumbs

Preheat oven to 325°. Spray 9 x 13 baking dish with nonstick cooking spray. Boil pasta as directed on package. Drain. Melt butter in heavy sauté pan, and whisk in flour and salt, just until golden brown. Add pepper to taste. Add cubed American cheese, blending until melted. Add shredded cheddar, and blend until melted. Add cooked macaroni and toss to coat. Spread mixture into prepared baking dish and sprinkle top with bread crumbs. Freeze if desired. Before baking, thaw completely. Bake uncovered for 1 hour or until knife comes out clean when inserted.

2 | The Family Meal: Why Bother?

Strange to see how a good dinner
and feasting reconciles everybody.

SAMUEL PEPYS

IT IS SO REWARDING when you hear your children's friends say to them something like, "I hear your mom makes the best chicken enchiladas"—and they haven't even been to your house for dinner.

That happened one night at Stephanie's house. She and her husband, Vern, along with fifteen-year-old Mitchel, had another family with two teenagers join them for a weeknight dinner. The conversation started with a pretty commonplace question—What are you learning in school?—but that opened up an American history conversation that seemed to include everyone. Coincidentally, both dads had just read a biography of John Adams, and they became animated with information themselves while the kids were joining in with random facts and questions.

"Did you know that he was the first president to live in the White House," said Mitchel, "and it was still under construction?"

"He's also one of the few influential presidents who do not appear on any of our money," said one of the dads.

"Why doesn't he?" another asked.

As the chicken enchilada course wound down, Stephanie served dessert, and the conversation continued. In fact, the conversation carried through the entire evening. Nobody even thought of turning on the television. Nobody was checking a smartphone or texting another friend. Everyone was tuned in to the conversation that had started over dinner and continued way beyond dessert.

There are some nights when you know that all the hassle of getting the whole family around the table for a meal is worth it. And then there are the others—the times you wonder why you even bother. In this chapter we'll show you why your family meal is worth the effort.

Did You Know?
Sixty-one percent of kids say their parents are more relaxed and fun to be around when they all have dinner together.

THE TENOR OF THE HOME

It used to be that people in our profession—psychologists and family therapists—would ask clients to describe their childhood family dinnertimes. It was a relatively quick and reliable way to determine the general tenor of a home. We would even ask them to draw the shape of the table and to place themselves, their parents, and their siblings around it. We'd have them describe a typical mealtime, including topics of conversation.

Some clients would recall many details and evoke word pictures of engaging interactions. Some would recall only vague and fleeting memories. Their childhood gatherings around the dinner table were either non-existent or nearly irrelevant. Back in that day, therapists saw a strong relationship between the love in a home and the richness of the family dinner table.

Of course, that was back in the Norman Rockwell era, when Mom cooked, Dad carved, Son cleared, and Daughter did the dishes. It was the era when June Cleaver wore pearls with her apron and Ward was in a sweater and tie. The table was set, the napkins were linen, the kids were scrubbed, and steam rose from the green-bean casserole.

WHAT WE DO AT DINNERTIME

Most popular activities at dinnertime, according to a recent survey:

- Watch TV shows/videos: 36 percent
- Talk with family/friends: 31 percent
- Just eat/drink: 27 percent
- Relax: 8 percent[1]

But sometime during the 1970s the question counselors had asked their clients in previous decades about their childhood dinner tables became more and more irrelevant.

The tidy picture of the Norman Rockwell dinner hour faded, and family dining fell dramatically over the next thirty years. With both parents working and the kids shuttling between sports practices or sitting glued to their computer screens at home, finding a time for everyone to sit around the same table, eat the same food, and listen to one another became more quaint than customary. Family dinners were now discretionary. And cooking them was drudgery. The popularity of the microwave oven meant that time spent standing in front of a stove was time wasted.

The revolutionary social, economic, and technological changes in family lifestyles in the last quarter of the 1900s made the therapeutic question obsolete. But that's no longer the case. In professional circles, the question is coming back because the results of a mountain of research are emerging, and the mysterious value of a consistent family dinner hour can no longer be ignored.

Did You Know?
Sixty-five percent of parents agree with this statement:
"My spouse and I generally feel less stressed when
we eat dinner together as a family."
Seventy percent of kids agree with this statement:
"I appreciate my parents more when we take time
to share a meal together."

WHY THE FAMILY MEAL IS WORTH IT
"What's for dinner?"

That's perhaps the most common—and, for some,

nightmare-inducing—question posed in households seven days a week, 365 days a year. It sends many moms reeling or—worse—straight to the nearest fast-food chain or take-out joint. Does that really matter?

Consider this: study after study shows that the more often families eat together, the less likely the kids are to smoke, drink, do drugs, get depressed, develop eating disorders, become overweight, and consider suicide—and the more likely they are to eat their vegetables, know which fork to use, learn big words, do well in school, feel that their parents love them, and delay having sex. And that's just for starters.

Let's take a look at four of the most-compelling reasons for taking a proactive position on the ritual of a family dinner hour.

Eating Together Means Eating Better

"Life expectancy would grow by leaps and bounds," says journalist Doug Larson, "if green vegetables smelled as good as bacon." He has a point. Eating what's good for us isn't always easy. That's why the nutritional bump that comes when a family dines together is such a bonus.

Let's start with the basics: *Eating together means eating better*. Tina and Stephanie say, "We believe that children will succeed in life as a result of engaging with their families in a way that causes them to feel loved, nurtured, and valued. We have seen in our families that there is no better time to do this than when we share our experiences and values while gathered around the dinner table." But this isn't just someone's opinion. It's a fact.

Studies show that families who eat together eat more healthfully.

For example, in a study that followed sixty-five children over a period of eight years, Harvard researchers looked at which activities—play, story time, events with family members, and other factors—most fostered healthy child development. When the data was analyzed, family dinners won out. The same researchers revealed that children who ate family dinners most days consumed far more fruits and vegetables and fewer fried foods, fats, and sodas than children who ate dinner with family members infrequently. Children who ate dinners with family members most days also had substantially higher intakes of dietary fiber, calcium, iron, folic acid, and all the vitamins a nutritionist could wish for.[2] Another study found that when children ate with their families, they used more low-fat practices, such as trimming fat from meat and using low-fat foods at meals.[3]

Developing good eating habits early on can help children be healthier for the rest of their lives.[4] Studies have even found that children who ate family dinners more frequently had more healthy eating habits when they were eating away from home.[5]

So if good nutrition is high on your priority list for your children, a routine family dinner hour is one way to make it easier to reach that goal.

Eating Together Gets Better with Practice
Oprah Winfrey conducted a "Family Dinner Experiment" some years ago on her talk show.[6] Five families volunteered to accept the challenge to eat dinner together every night

for a month, staying at the table for a minimum of a half hour each time. As part of the experiment, all family members kept journals to record their feelings about the experience. At the beginning of the experiment, sharing meals was a chore for many of the families, and the minutes at the table dragged. But by the end of the month, all the families were happy and planned to continue dining together most evenings, if not every night.

That experience—of a slow start to a shared dinnertime—is typical, which is why some families give eating together a whirl only to find that it doesn't work so well for them initially and therefore give up. In reality, however, it's more likely that they just didn't give it enough time. If they had, they would have discovered what the families in Oprah's experiment found: in about a month's time the family dinner hour morphed from a chore to something they looked forward to. Of course, we don't need to rely on just five families on

> ## Supper is about nourishment of all kinds.
>
> MIRIAM WEINSTEIN

a television show to make the case. Studies of countless families back up this point. In one of those studies, conducted at Columbia University, researchers who had been gathering data for almost ten years found that the less often family members gather and eat together, the worse the experience is when they do. But for those families who give it a fighting chance and eat together at least three evenings a week for a month, the family dinner hour does indeed get better with practice.[7] So if you've tried it before and you're thinking that this whole idea of eating together as a family is not for you, you just might need to try it a little longer.

Eating Together Is Something Your Kids Want

"One of the biggest fears moms have about starting a regular family dinnertime," says Tina, "is that they are dragging their kids into something they don't want to do. Moms think this will cause their kids to resent them—but just the opposite is true."

The reality is that teens who have frequent family dinners are almost three times as likely to say they have an excellent relationship with their mothers and three times as likely to say they have an excellent relationship with their fathers. The teens are also more than twice as likely to report that their parents are very good at listening to them.

Teens themselves understand the value of family dinners. Nearly three-quarters of teens think that eating dinner together with their parents is important. And get this: most teens (60 percent) who have dinner with their parents fewer than five nights a week wish they could eat dinner with their parents more often. Further, in contrast to teens who don't have family dinnertimes, those who do are more likely to think frequent family dinners are important and to want to have them more often.[8]

The bottom line is that once you carve a groove into your family schedule for dinnertime together, your kids, regardless of their ages, want it more than you might ever imagine.

Eating Together Is about Far More Than Food

"To be honest, the reason our first group of moms got together for our assemble-and-freeze parties was simply to save time and have a wholesome meal for our kids instead of fast food," says Stephanie. "The benefit of what that time around the table was doing in our families wasn't even on the agenda until we discovered it."

Stephanie is referring to the magic that occurs within a family when mealtime becomes a ritual of togetherness. It's not about the food on the table; it's not even about the conversations around it. Rather, there's an unidentifiable bond that grows stronger when family members eat together. Why? Because this time-tested ritual helps families cultivate the six qualities that make a home the safest place on earth (see the list of those qualities in chapter 1).

Think about it: *commitment* is a given when every member of the family carves out time to be at dinner. It may mean missing a practice or not scheduling a business call, but regardless of the adjustments that need to be made, commitment is synonymous with a regular dinnertime. *Affection* and *appreciation* also come into play at the dinner table. Once families learn to leverage this time in the most meaningful way they can, gratitude emerges—whether it's for the meal itself or for anything else. Of course, *positive communication* and *time together* are the centerpieces of this ritual. Three in four teens report that they talk to their parents about what's going on in their lives during dinner, and eight in ten parents agree that, by having family dinner

THE HOUR THAT MATTERS MOST

together, they learn more about what's going on in their teens' lives.

Spiritual well-being, too, is heightened for families who focus on it. A simple and short word of grace before the meal, for example, speaks volumes about the values a family holds. And the *ability to cope with stress* also increases for families using this practice. A Jewish proverb goes, "Worries go down better with soup," and Miguel de Cervantes is said to have quipped, "All sorrows are less with bread."

All of the six "secrets" to creating the safest place on earth are nourished through a shared and routine ritual of a family dinner hour. There is something in the nature of eating together that forms a bond between people. Even the word *companion* is derived from the Latin words meaning "with bread." Meals become more meaningful, more powerful than we ever imagined, when we share them regularly with our families. Especially in this day and age, it is one of the few times when a family can sit down together and speak face-to-face. Dining together relaxes our spirits, joins our souls, and makes

WHAT MAKES YOUR TEENAGER HAPPY?

What makes someone between the ages of 13 and 24 happy is not what you might think, according to an extensive survey conducted by the Associated Press and MTV.[9] The results showed that spending time with family (73 percent) makes young people happiest. Nearly half of kids surveyed mentioned one of their parents as their hero, with mothers (29 percent) ranking higher than fathers (21 percent). After family, "relationships with friends" was most likely to make children happy.

us more loving. It's what caused famed playwright Oscar Wilde to say, "After a good dinner one can forgive anybody, even one's own relations."

Try This

Family dinners are not necessarily primarily about the food but about the company and the conversation. If there's no other option, you can connect just as well over delivery pizza some nights as you can over something homemade, as long as you gather to enjoy the time together as you eat.

FAMILY MEALS

"Kids who dine with the folks are healthier, happier, and better students, which is why a dying tradition is coming back," says a report in *Time* magazine. The article was based on an in-depth study conducted by the National Center on Addiction and Substance Abuse at Columbia University—a study whose research consisted of nearly a decade of gathering data.

After sifting through the raw data, researchers identified several important patterns. For example, 55 percent of twelve-year-olds say they have dinner with a parent every night, compared with only 26 percent of seventeen-year-olds. Along ethnic lines, 54 percent of Hispanic teens say they eat with a parent most nights, compared with 40 percent of African American teens and 39 percent of white teens.

The study also clearly defined the benefits of eating meals as a family. Children who most often eat meals with their parents are 40 percent more likely to say they get mainly As and Bs in school than kids who have two or fewer family dinners a week. In addition, children who participate in family meals fewer than three times a week are more than twice as likely to say there is a great deal of tension among family members and are much less likely to think their parents are proud of them.

Finally, the study showed a correlation between the frequency and quality of family meals. For example, among those who eat together three or fewer times a week, 45 percent say the TV is on during meals (as opposed to 37 percent of all households), and nearly one-third say there isn't much conversation.[10]

> **TRUE OR FALSE?**
> As kids get into their teen years, they're less willing to be part of family dinners.
> Answer: False. When it comes to ranking the importance of eating together at home versus engaging in other activities, there is no difference between kids ages 8 to 12 and kids ages 13 to 18.

STILL NOT CONVINCED?

If you're still not convinced that a family meal is worth the effort, you may be held up on one primary issue—time. Your schedule won't allow it, right? *I'd like to prepare a home-style meal for my family*, you may be thinking, *but I can't even find time to go grocery shopping.* You're not alone. Conflicting schedules and busyness are the top reasons people give for not initiating the ritual of a shared family meal.

"I get that," says Tina. "Time was the biggest hurdle

I had for not instituting family dinner in our home. After all, I was a working mom who wasn't free to shop and cook all afternoon. By the time I got home, I was exhausted. I was doing well just to scrounge up a frozen pizza or some chicken nuggets for the kids. On top of that, my kids were finicky eaters and rarely wanted the same thing to eat."

If you can relate, we want to share with you one more reason to give the hour that matters most a serious effort. And this reason doesn't have to do with your kids. It has everything to do with you.

On top of all the dinnertime studies over the past decade that have shown a myriad of payoffs for your kids, newer studies are showing payoffs for parents as well— especially for moms who work outside the home. How can that be? The fact is, this family ritual reduces conflict and strain that result from working long hours. It's true. "Parents, not just kids, benefit from time spent eating together," says Jenet Jacob of Brigham Young University and lead author of one study. She looked at 1,580 working mothers who were putting in long hours on the job. But guess what? When these time-starved and stressed-out moms made room for a routine family dinner, they reported less stress and strain for themselves and their households. When they made it home in time for dinner with their families, they felt greater personal success as well as success in relationships with their spouses and kids. They even felt more kindly toward their workplaces. In some cases, these women experienced greater benefits than anyone else in the family. "It is noteworthy," says

Jacob, "that although longer work hours predicted significantly greater perception of success in work life, work interference with dinnertime predicted lower perception of success in work life."[11] That's astounding!

> If more of us valued food and cheer and song above hoarded gold, it would be a merrier world.
>
> J. R. R. TOLKIEN

Now, we're not saying that having family dinners is the answer to all your problems. We're not saying it eliminates all your stress. Far from it. But we are saying that everyone—including you—wins when you get into the rhythm of this ritual. You don't have to live a carefree life with a casual schedule or have extraordinary homemaking skills to pull this off. And nobody's asking you to take a culinary course. You don't even need to be überorganized, because a family dinner—even a hassled one—is better for mothers, as well as the rest of the family, than no family dinner. The point is that even if you work long hours and shuttle your kids from one activity to the next, you can still reap the amazing benefits of the hour that matters most.

FROM STEPHANIE

When I was about ten years old, my mother went back to work, and she came up with a new strategy for getting us together around the dinner table. She assigned each member of the family one night of the week to make dinner. Can you believe it? Mom cooked on Monday nights. I had Tuesday nights. My younger brother had Wednesday nights—which usually meant peanut butter sandwiches and apples. And my dad had Thursday nights, which almost always meant we were going out. On Friday nights we were each on our own for dinner.

I give Mom all the credit for letting me develop my cooking skills so young. On the following page is one of my favorite childhood recipes.

Super Simple Sloppy Joes

1 pound lean ground beef
1 package dry onion soup mix
1 cup marinara sauce
1 cup barbecue sauce
6 hamburger buns

In a large frying pan, brown ground beef 10 to 12 minutes over medium-high heat. Line a dinner plate with paper towels and place cooked beef on it to drain. In the same pan, blend sauces and onion soup mix. Add cooked beef and simmer on low 10 to 20 minutes. If preparing for freezer, cool completely and place in sealed container in the freezer, then warm mixture on stove top. Serve in hamburger buns.

3 | Recovering the Lost Art of Eating Together

In the span of one generation, regular family meals have disappeared from our cultural landscape.

MIRIAM WEINSTEIN

"KIDS, THANK YOUR MOTHER for driving to the store and getting this." Do you recognize this line? If you've read Michael Lewis's book *The Blind Side* or seen the movie by the same title, starring Sandra Bullock, you can't forget it.

Michael Oher, a homeless African-American teenager who grew up in the poverty-stricken projects of Memphis, had few options and even fewer opportunities. But that was before he crossed paths with an unstoppable force in the person of Leigh Anne Tuohy. What follows is a series of events that are difficult to believe—but they are true.

Michael, a six-foot-four-inch, 310-pound behemoth, is taken in by the Tuohys, a wealthy family who nurtures his abilities and helps him find healing and a hidden talent for football that eventually leads to a professional career.

One scene early in the film shows Michael's first weekend with the Tuohys. It's Thanksgiving. As the family is grabbing food and jostling for space among the seats in the family room in front of not one but two separate televisions broadcasting football games, Sean Tuohy, the father, says with a smile, "Kids, thank your mother for driving to the store and getting this."

Michael, who has never had a family to speak of, let alone a Thanksgiving dinner, goes into the formal dining room with his plate of food and sits by himself. He has never sat at a family dinner table in his life but, almost by instinct, knows that sitting at that table represents all the things about family he's never had but always knew he wanted.

Leigh Anne sees Michael at the table alone and herds the family into the dining room to eat around the table with Michael.

"Why are we in here?" one of the kids grouses.

"Shh!" says Leigh Anne. "Shall we say grace?"

The family holds hands, and Leigh Anne Tuohy prays, "Heavenly Father, we thank you for all the many blessings on this family. We thank you for bringing us a new friend. And we ask that you look after us in this holiday season that we may never forget how very fortunate we are. Amen."

Sean then turns to his young son and asks, "SJ, the score?"

"Up by ten."

"Can you pass me the green beans, please?"

"Don't pick it with your fingers, just take a spoon."

Leigh Anne says to her son, "Elbows!"

Clearly, in many families, eating together is a lost art. Even a family of means with a room in the house dedicated to "dining" struggles with the idea of having a meal around a common table and no television (even on Thanksgiving, in the Tuohy house). Less than 40 percent of American families are eating together at dinner, a figure down substantially from the 1970s.[1]

That's why we dedicate this chapter to recovering the fundamentals of family dining—and we do mean fundamentals! We're talking about the kitchen and how to convert it from a place where you "heat and eat" your food to a place where you create a nightly occasion of togetherness. Of course, if you've got plenty of cooking experience under your belt, feel free to skip the parts that don't pertain to your situation. But if you'd like some encouragement in the kitchen, we'll begin with a few basics and then give you some pointers for setting the mood as well as the table.

COOK AS IF YOU MEAN IT

While it's true that the biggest hurdles to enjoying a family dinner hour are busyness and conflicting schedules, the next complaint on the table is, "I don't know *how* to create a family meal." Because of the widespread availability of convenience foods, already-prepared foods, and quick-serve restaurants, the tricks of the cooking trade are rarely passed down from generation to generation these days. Of course, not every meal needs to be prepared at home for a family to enjoy it together, but when we *do* cook, we may do so with fear and trepidation.

Sometimes we tiptoe around in the kitchen out of respect or deference to someone else. Maybe our mothers made it better, so we don't want to touch those signature dishes. Or we've been frightened by the "food police," who have scared us into thinking we might poison our families by undercooking eggs, using a harmful cooking pan, or letting uncooked chicken touch the wrong cutting board. Sometimes we slave away on a dish that the family doesn't like. And sometimes things go terribly wrong: the bread we tried to bake comes out as a doorstop.

Whatever the reasons you are afraid, you need to overcome your fear of cooking. You don't need to emulate Julia Child. You just need to learn some basics. "Once I learned that good cooking stems from using fresh, seasonal ingredients," says Tina, "my anxiety in the kitchen reduced significantly. You really don't need to do much to make fresh food taste good. A little salt, a little olive oil, and you're cooking!"

The important point to keep in mind is that everyone started somewhere. People aren't born with a wooden cooking spoon and a spatula in their tiny fists. Even the great Julia Child said, "I was thirty-two when I started cooking; up until then, I just ate." So let go of the guilt and keep your head high as you're learning to cook.

COOKING 101

Cooking has come a long way from when our ancestors roasted wild game and local vegetation over an open fire. We've discovered an infinite number of ways to prepare and season food; in fact, entire television networks devote themselves to it. But somewhere between master-ing the rudiments and building cakes that look like city skylines, most of us have lost touch with cooking. It used to be that every cook knew what it meant to sauté or sear or "add flour to thicken." Today, not so much. So the fol-lowing few thoughts are specifi-cally for the beginner.

First, *find recipes that work for you.* You don't have to cook everything, just the dishes your family enjoys most. That's why we've supplied some fresh and easy recipes at the end of each chapter. These are tried and true, sure to please a wide variety of tastes. Friends and relatives are great sources of recipes too.

> Food is not about impressing people. It's about making them feel comfortable.
>
> INA GARTEN

Next, *get equipped.* This means gathering the ingredients and the tools you'll need. When you're starting out, don't substitute ingre-dients in recipes. You can do that once you have more experience and can better predict how a particular sub-stitution might change the taste or texture. And don't eyeball the amounts of ingredients. Have a set of mea-suring spoons and cups, and use them. In addition, every basic kitchen should have a good chef's knife.

The pros call this step *"mise en place."* The term means getting everything you need—both your tools and all ingredients—together so you don't end up with something missing at a critical point in the cooking process. You can do this before you even turn on the stove. And speaking of your stove, learn the different degrees used in heating water—many recipes require water as part of the process. *Poaching* is a lower, gentle heat and is usually the method used with delicate foods such as fish or eggs. *Simmering* is a little hotter, with a few small bubbles rising to the surface, and is usually used for sauces and foods that need a long time to cook (spaghetti sauce or soups, for example). When water is *boiling*, it gets as hot as it's going to get and begins to evaporate into steam. One other note: when it comes to preheating your oven, be patient with the time it takes to reach the desired temperature, or you'll throw off your cooking times.

When possible, taste your dishes frequently while you cook (exceptions are raw or partially cooked fish, meat, or eggs because of food-safety issues). This lets you make sure the balance of spices is correct and also helps you to learn how flavors develop with cooking.

Of course, we are barely even beginning to scratch the surface here. You'll learn more as you try new recipes, ask friends, and visit a cooking shop or two. The bottom line is not to be intimidated. Learning to prepare a meal is easier than you think.

SETTING THE MOOD WHILE SETTING THE TABLE

After years of practice, the Woodruffs have family dinners down to a science, and what they do has worked ever since their children, now late adolescents, were toddlers. They start most evenings around six, but they're flexible if they know someone is going to be late. While Mom is preparing the meal, one of the kids gets out the place mats (or sometimes a tablecloth); puts the dishes, glasses, and silverware on the table; and arranges them with confidence, knowing that the fork goes on the left and the knife and spoon are on the right. Another child lights a candle or two on the table, and Dad lowers the lights with the dimmer switch.

By the way, the Woodruffs' routine doesn't require repeated calling to come to dinner. That is bound to start any meal off on a negative note. Because the mealtime is fixed and predictable, family members know when to start gathering. In fact, the conversations typically begin in the preparation process. But if somebody hasn't shown up yet, one call will do the trick.

That's it. Over the years, the Woodruffs have found their groove, and it works. Dinnertime is comfortable and relaxing. They stay at the table until each person is finished. And since Mom prepared the meal, Dad and the kids (now that they are older) clean up. Everyone pitches in, and everyone feels connected.

After years of trial and error, Mom and Dad have learned what topics of conversation to avoid, too. They steer clear of problem-solving talks that are likely to get intense, and instead of hassling the kids about their eating habits, they have one simple rule: the kids have to try everything that's served to them, but they can decline to finish anything they don't like by saying, "I think I've had enough for now." No cajoling. No threats. And no rules about cleaning their plates. For the Woodruffs, trying to enforce that expectation just isn't worth it.

They also have a few routines that make their weekly process easier. On Friday evenings, for example, they almost always make homemade pizza together. And on most Sundays, Dad typically makes brunch, which includes his highly anticipated Danish pancakes.

Is every meal at the Woodruff home perfect? Of course not. Sometimes Dad rushes the meal to get to some pressing work. Sometimes Mom feels frazzled after working all day and discovering that she doesn't have an important ingredient she thought was on hand for that evening's meal. That's when they order takeout—but they still light the candles and lower the lights. Why? Because they value the bond that's built from this family ritual and they know that the little touches they use to create something special make a big difference.

Of course, you don't have to do everything the Woodruffs do to create a great dining experience. Every family finds its own way on this path. But those who do it well consider the mood as well as the food. And the reason is simple: the pleasure of eating at a beautiful table—whether or not it includes candles, relaxing music, or flowers—helps make any meal more enjoyable and connecting. The point is that the dining experience involves more than merely ingesting food. It also is a setting for maximizing positive conversations.

> Whether you are eating on china or paper plates, the table time with your loved ones is what matters most. No guilt should creep into your mind if something is not homemade—it's the time invested in eating together that you can be proud of.
>
> STEPHANIE ALLEN

Light Up Your Life

A friend shared the following great advice with me when my kids were young, and I have never forgotten it. Her six-year-old son was a handful, very energetic. One autumn evening she lit an apple-and-cinnamon scented candle. When she called her rambunctious boy for dinner, he abruptly stopped in his tracks and asked, "Are you making an apple pie?" She showed him the candle, and he asked if they could put it on the dinner table. Of course, she did. The soft light and flicker of the flame provided a focal point for her busy son. It was relaxing, soothing, and calming. It was one of the best dinners they had ever had together. From then on my friend lit a dinner candle every night. Simple efforts can have big benefits.

AVOID THE TWO BIGGEST PITFALLS

Before we leave this chapter, we need to tell you what happens in some families who set out with good intentions to create a ritual of family dining but give up before it sticks. They fall prey to two pitfalls that trip them up.

Pitfall 1: Treating Your Kitchen like a Food Court

Meander through any American shopping center, and you're bound to eventually find a food court, an area with multiple food vendors and a common seating area for eating. It's likely to have all the usual fast-food vendors catering to shoppers on the go. The second-floor food court at the Paramus Park shopping mall, which opened in New Jersey in 1974, has been credited with being the first successful food court. But wherever the idea of food courts started, it needs to end in your kitchen.

Consider this all-too-common scenario: sometime between five thirty and six thirty in the evening, a teenage daughter wanders into the kitchen and asks Mom, "What's for dinner?" Mom gives a few options that are quick and easy. She has some chicken tenders, a frozen pizza, hot dogs, and a couple of frozen dinners she can put in the microwave.

"What sounds good?" Mom asks.

That's when the girl stands in front of the open refrigerator, makes her selection, and asks Mom to prepare it. She leans on the counter, flipping through a magazine until the whir of the microwave ends with a ding.

"It's ready," Mom says.

About that time, the girl's younger brother wanders in. "What are you guys eating?"

"Your sister's having pot pie. Would you like one?" Mom asks.

"What else do we have?" he questions.

You get the picture. This mom has turned her kitchen into a food court, serving each family member individually, usually at the counter on a stool, and none of them ever reaps the reward of a ritual that brings everyone around the table together for a shared meal.

Here's the point: when it comes to dinner, your kids are not your customers. They don't need to have their own meals. While you might think that catering to their individual whims is showing love and care, it's more likely instilling a subtle attitude in your kids that says, *My immediate needs take precedence over any needs of the family.* Don't let that happen. As you prepare and serve a common meal, they'll eventually see the value in the shared experience.

Pitfall 2: Keeping Your TV on during the Meal

Chances are you've not attended a Scottish bagpipe competition, but if you have, you most likely noticed something peculiar at the judges' table. On occasion, you'd have seen some of the judges covering their ears, which doesn't seem to make sense. They are, after all, there specifically to listen to and judge the music. But inflated bagpipes naturally make a steady droning noise. The actual music is played over and above the drone. So by covering their ears, the judges shut out some of the low-pitched droning to focus more on the higher-pitched melody.

A similar situation arises in homes where the television is on, even in the background, while family members are at the dinner table. The undercurrent of television noise can't help but distract them from hearing one another clearly. The television is a killer to the underlying purpose of the family meal. Fortunately, we don't have to cover our ears. We can simply turn off the tube. Of course, that's not easy for some households.

We noted earlier that less than 40 percent of American families are eating dinner together. What we didn't mention was that about half of them have the television on in the background during dinnertime. And a third of these families eat in front of the television, where the extent of their conversation consists of comments such as, "Shh," "What else is on?" and "Where's the ketchup?"[2]

The average American household has a television on for approximately eight hours and fourteen minutes every day.[3] Turning it off for an hour during dinner is not a huge sacrifice. Of course, there's no need to be legalistic about it. Some families make an occasional event out of eating together while watching something special, such as the Olympic games. Some have a weekend dinner/movie night. The goal, however, is to keep television and family dining separate except for special events. The same holds true for reading the paper, texting, and phoning. If these distractions are not set aside during your meals together, you'll never have an environment that's conducive to conversation and connection.

FROM STEPHANIE
Throughout history women often got together to share a chore. In ancient days they went to the well to get the family water (the chore), but by going at the same time, they could visit and catch up on one another's lives. In the early 1800s women started quilting bees. They needed to make quilts for their families (the chore), and what better way than to make quilts together so they could talk and enjoy one another's company. For me, getting together with my busy friend once a month and making dinners for our freezers was the one time we could get the chore done and still have time to visit all day, sharing parenting tips and cooking ideas, as well as indulging in plain old girl-time therapy!

In fact, that's exactly how Dream Dinners came about. My girlfriend and I were making our fix-and-freeze dinners for the month and were talking about all the other friends who wanted us to show them how to make these types of dinners. We didn't quite end up with a business plan written on a napkin, but the idea for Dream Dinners was created while we were assembling our own frozen meals for the month.

FROM TINA

My sister Kim would travel two hours to my home for the weekend and stay with me. My husband, Scott, would take the kids to do something for the day, and Kim and I would take over the entire kitchen and assemble dinners. At the end of the day, our backs were aching, but looking at the stacks of food we had before us, we agreed that this was the best thing we had ever done for our families. And we so much enjoyed our conversations throughout the day and the time we spent together.

WINNING THE FOOD FIGHT

In the Canadian Northlands there are just two seasons: winter and July. When the back roads begin to thaw, they become so muddy that vehicles leave deep ruts, which

THE SISTERHOOD OF THE TRAVELING MEAL

Frozen, assembled dinners travel well. Give them to friends and families in need or as a thank-you gift. Take them with you to condos, camping trips, cabins, and family holidays away from home. I have even taken them on airline flights, packed right in my suitcase. There's no need to worry about ice—it's cold where checked luggage is kept. It is easy to take a home-cooked frozen dinner almost anywhere you go.

freeze when cold weather returns. For those entering this primitive area during the winter months, there is a sign that reads, "Driver, please choose carefully which rut you drive in, because you'll be in it for the next twenty miles."

The same holds true for the proverbial ruts we fall into as families. And if our routine doesn't include a predictable time of dining together, we tend to stay in that rut until we realize one day that the kids are grown and gone and the family meal never happened.

There's no denying it—we live fast. That's why meals are consumed in the car, at the gym, at work, at play, and at staggered times from other family members at home. But it doesn't have to be that way. You can carve a new groove into your family's routine.

If you can barely remember the last time your family gathered around the table for dinner with the television off, we know this is going to be a challenge. But we also know that it's going to be easier than you think. The keys to bringing family dinners back are to stick with it and to facilitate meal preparation by planning and assembling entrees ahead of time. In fact, near the end of this book we will give you a step-by-step approach for trying this fix-and-freeze routine and making it a success.

TINA'S TIME OFF

When I was in school, once in a while my mother would surprise me with a day off, a "hooky day." We would go to a movie or shopping and then head to the small town of Snohomish, which happens to be the same small town where I now live. We'd go to Cabbage Patch

Restaurant—our favorite—for lunch. And each time we'd order the same delicious Hearty Cabbage Patch Soup. Cabbage Patch Restaurant is still in business, and I tend to make the soup at home a few times each year. It always brings back special memories for me because it was on those hooky days that Mom and I had some of our best talks. In fact, the same holds true these days when I serve Hearty Garden Patch Soup to my kids.

Hearty Garden Patch Soup

1½ to 2 pounds hamburger or Italian sausage
4 to 5 stalks celery, diced
½ medium onion, diced

Brown these 3 ingredients in a large skillet.

1 can (28 oz) diced tomatoes
2 cans (14 oz each) beef broth
2 cans (16 oz each) dark red kidney beans (including liquid)
2 cans (15 oz each) tomato sauce
½ medium head of cabbage cut into bite-size pieces
¼ teaspoon chili powder
salt and pepper to taste

Combine all ingredients, including browned hamburger or sausage, in a large kettle. Simmer for 1 to 2 hours. If you are going to freeze the recipe, cool completely, then pour into a container, seal it, and place in freezer. Warm on stove top when ready to serve.

Helpful hints: If you're in a hurry, you may boil the soup for 20 minutes and serve. For larger quantities, add another can each of beef broth and tomato sauce. Good served with corn bread.

DREAM DINNERS.

HOMEMADE, MADE EASY

Congratulations on winning a copy of "The Hour That Matters Most," and thank you for being a loyal Dream Dinners customer! #DreamDinners #HomemadeMadeEasy

4 | The Heart of Great Table Talk

A mother understands what a child does not say.

JEWISH PROVERB

FROM STEPHANIE

When our daughter Karlene was in first grade, she posed an intriguing question at the dinner table: "I don't like it when the boys chase me on the playground. How do I get them to stop?" The answer we gave her then is the same answer we discussed throughout the years, just applied to different situations. "Stop running." It's an easy lesson for a child to hear, but it can take a lifetime to learn.

Over the dinner table, conversations grow and mature just as our kids do. As we teach life lessons, I am reminded that I, too, need to stop running so that problems can't chase me. Challenging situations and circumstances are always going to be a part of our lives, but how we react to them reveals who we are.

■ ■ ■

Our little Jackson, the younger of two brothers, loves to talk. If you ask him about his day, be prepared to take a seat. He'll typically unpack *all* the details, describing step-by-step the sequence of his day at school. When he was just three years old, he'd pepper us with questions on an otherwise quiet car ride: "Why do they call it golf?" "Do worms have ears?" Now eight, Jackson still doesn't shy away from questions: "What do you think it's really like in hell?"—*Whoa!* Didn't see that one coming!—or "Why do we have countries?"

For the most part, we love Jack's questions. But from time to time, when we're too preoccupied with something else to give him an immediate response, Jack will pose a question that hangs in silence. And then, as if he's just delivered a joke that bombed in a New York comedy club, he'll say with a rise in his voice, "Anybody?"

We laugh every time. Why? Because we know just how he feels. Haven't you sometimes wondered if anyone out there is listening? We all know the feeling, but not all of us have the confidence or presence of mind to blurt out, "Anyone?"

Our older son, John, doesn't. He isn't as chatty as his younger brother. In fact, sometimes we have to really work just to get John to speak up. If we don't, he can be content to process his day internally without really saying much at all. But even Jack, with all his verbalizing, doesn't necessarily say what we need to understand. That's why table talk is so essential. It's the centerpiece of every great family dinner. The key, of course, is to get your kids talking.[1]

WHAT IF YOU COULD BUY IT?

Suppose you could pick up a product at your local drugstore, take the bottle home, and spray the contents as an indiscernible mist around your family's dinner table. It would instantly set the stage for some of the greatest conversations your family has ever had. This little bottle would allow you and everyone else at the table to speak freely because there would be comfort and confidence in knowing that everyone would be understood. Not only that, it would also guarantee that everyone around the table would be suddenly more understanding toward the others. Can you imagine this? Whenever you used this little spray bottle, warm and inviting conversations would move naturally from uncontrollable laughter to deep and heartfelt vulnerability to connection. The table would provide a safe and comfortable setting where everyone could relax and feel safe, accepted, and loved.

If such a product were to exist, it would surely consist of just one ingredient: *empathy*—the capacity we humans have, when we try, to put ourselves in someone else's shoes and see the world from his or her perspective. That's all, 100 percent empathy. If you could bottle it and dispense it around every dinner hour, you would have pretty much all you'd need. Why? Because empathy is at the heart of all great table talk. Of course, you can't pick up a bottle of empathy at your local pharmacy. But if you want to get your kids talking, you've got to find it somewhere. Thankfully, you can find it within yourself. And think of the rewards when you do! Imagine what a good dose of empathy would do for your family when it comes to opening up your children's spirit and enjoying conversations together.

If each of your family members could see the world from one another's point of view instantly and routinely, what would your dinner hour look like?

> # Some of the most important conversations I've ever had occurred at my family's dinner table.
>
> BOB EHRLICH

Chances are your dinnertime would have more laughter and less bickering. You'd become more adept at reading your children's facial expressions. You'd offer more care and comfort to one another. You'd use empathy to bring about more playfulness and fun with your kids. With an abundance of empathy, you'd have fewer hurt feelings and a lot more happiness. In short, you'd have more moments of deep, thoughtful understanding.

With more empathy around your dinner table, you'd find that your family would be more considerate and more indulgent of one another's quirks. You'd hear more compliments and feel more gratitude. Your children would feel safer. You'd find that everyone would be less judgmental and a lot more accepting. You'd probably also find that family members would offer one another more grace. You might even find that you'd hug one another longer and more often. You'd see more smiles. In short, you'd have more love.

This you can know for sure—empathy is at the heart of love. No other skill or practice can do more for your family than empathy. Yet too many parents neglect it at their peril, because they've never learned its priceless value.[2]

HOW CONNECTED ARE YOU?

The following short quiz is designed to get your wheels turning. Don't worry about trying to get the "right" answer; just give the answer that lines up with what you currently believe.

T F I know what my child most often daydreams about.
T F I know the best and worst part of my child's school day.
T F I know my child's greatest fear.
T F I know the names of my child's six closest friends and a little about their parents.
T F I am intentional about having a meaningful conversation with my child every day.

Scoring: If you answered "false" to any of these five items, it's time to brush up on empathy and how to have great table talk.

LIVING IN HARMONY

In 1885, poet Walt Whitman wrote his masterwork, *Leaves of Grass*. And in it, he has this telling line: "I do not ask the wounded person how he feels, I myself *become* the wounded person" (emphasis added). In a very real sense, empathy helps you *become your child—accurately seeing the world as he or she sees it.* It's important to note that when you empathize with a child, the empathy is almost always one sided. It's not reciprocal. That's why it's particularly challenging at times. But that's also why what we do is called parenting. We can't expect our children to give us much empathy in return. That ability comes only with maturity. And when it does, your connection to your child deepens in a way that you've not known before. Some call it *brilliance.* That spark of connection in that moment with your child is delightful and radiant. It's almost sacred—a family communion. Sure, you'll have glimpses of mutual empathy with your children here and there, but you can't expect it. Still, as the parent—as the mature one—you hold tremendous influence over the environment of your dinner table even when you alone put empathy into practice. Great conversations emerge when you empathize.

As we've said in our book *Trading Places*—an entire project we've devoted to empathy—we like to think of empathy as *attunement,* an idea that actually has musical connotations and means the state of being in tune or in harmony. And that's exactly what empathy does in our families. It enables us to be in tune with one another and to live in harmony. And what family doesn't want that?

THINK LIKE A FROG
When was the last time you read the famous Brothers Grimm tale "The Princess and the Frog"? The writers at *Sesame Street* must love it. We remember watching it together when Jackson was four. But rather than the typical

ending in which the spoiled princess kisses the frog (who then turns back into a prince), *Sesame Street*'s Miss Piggy, adorned with her jeweled tiara, doesn't find her prince with a kiss. Instead, with her kiss *she* becomes a frog!

That's all it took for Jackson to laugh without inhibition. But it was John, our then nine-year-old, who added a more serious observation: "If you want to know frogs, you've got to feel like a frog and think like a frog."[3] That's the idea of empathy in a nutshell.

LISTEN TO THIS

Every so often, when we are speaking at a marriage seminar somewhere around the country, we recount an experience we had when we were sitting on an airplane. Les turned to me and said, "Listen to this." He pulled down the tray table and, with eyes full of expectancy, began tapping on it with his index finger.

I listened for a moment, obviously puzzled.

He just kept tapping and looking at me.

"Have you lost your mind?" I asked as I put my magazine down.

"I'm tapping a song. Can you guess what it is?"

Les kept tapping as I halfheartedly played along.

"Come on, you can get this," he said.

That's when a curious passenger next to me, who had been completely quiet up to this point, piped up: "Is it Morse code?"

Les, suddenly self-conscious, terminated his tapping.

"Seriously, what's that all about?" I asked.

Les insisted it was a song and revealed that he'd been

reading about a research project at Stanford University that compelled him to try the experiment on me.

The study was unusually simple. Elizabeth Newton, a doctoral student, assigned people to one of two roles: "tapper" or "listener." A tapper received a list of a couple of dozen well-known songs such as "Happy Birthday to You," "Mary Had a Little Lamb," and "The Star-Spangled Banner." The task, after selecting one of the songs, was to tap out the rhythm on a table for a listener. The listener's job was to decipher the rhythm being tapped and guess the song.

Pretty simple, right? As it turns out, the listener's job is actually quite difficult—as the curious plane passenger and I discovered. Over the course of Newton's experiment, 120 songs were tapped out. Listeners correctly identified only 2.5 percent of the songs. That's just three correct guesses out of 120![4]

What does this atypical doctoral dissertation have to do with great table talk? Plenty. Before the listeners guessed the name of a song, Newton asked the tappers to predict the odds that their listeners would guess correctly. The tappers predicted that their listeners would be right 50 percent of the time. In other words, tappers thought they were getting their message across one time out of two tries. But in fact, their message was getting across only one time in forty tries.

Why the discrepancy? Because when tappers tap, they are *hearing* the song in their heads. The tapping seems obvious to them. They can't help but hear it as they tap, and they therefore believe that listeners have a very good chance of deciphering the tunes. Try it yourself. Tap "Happy Birthday to You." It's impossible to avoid hearing the tune as you do so. Then when the guess is "Mary Had a Little Lamb," you wonder, *How could my listener be so off?*

Of course, listeners are not dim witted. Not knowing what a tune is, they hear only a bunch of disconnected taps that resemble chicken pecks more than a musical number. But to an informed tapper, the listener comes off as dim witted.

The same thing happens in family conversations. When we "tap out" our message—whether we do it with words, inflection, or body language—we believe it should be relatively obvious to our "listening" family member. But it's not. Sometimes a seemingly evident message isn't evident at all. It's far from obvious if the listener is not in the know.

That's where the power of empathy comes in. Once you hone your abilities to put yourself in your child's shoes (or in your spouse's shoes, for that matter), you will "tap" differently. What's more, you'll "listen" differently. In fact, when you harness the power of empathy around the table, you'll enjoy a connection with one another like you've never had before.[5]

A FAILURE TO COMMUNICATE

Nearly every developmental psychologist will recount a common occurrence to illustrate how self-focused children typically are. Here's how it goes: little Suzy gets a phone call from her father. He asks her if Mommy is home. Instead of saying yes, Suzy nods her head. *Incredible*, you say? Not if you're little Suzy. Her father, hearing no response, asks again, and in reply, Suzy again nods. Of course, what Suzy does not realize is that her father, on the other end of the line, is completely unable to see her nodding. They're not using smartphones with cameras. Just voices. But Suzy can see things only from her own perspective. *I'm nodding my head*, she says to herself. *Why do you keep asking me the same question?*[6]

Of course, as we mature, we eventually learn to look beyond ourselves and consider another person's perspective. But the basic inclination to see the world only from our view stays with us. Even as adults we become puzzled or frustrated when another person doesn't see, hear, or understand something the way we do. That's when we have a failure to communicate, and family members complain, "You don't understand me" or "You're not listening" or "We just don't talk anymore."

IT'S ALL ABOUT PERSPECTIVE

Putting ourselves in our children's shoes has everything to do with seeing the world from their perspective. And that's the rub. As adults we want them to see the world from our perspective. Consider the following:

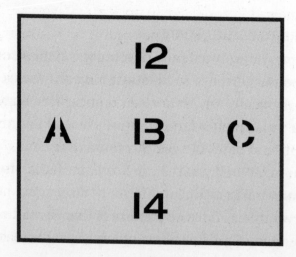

If you're focusing on the column that starts with 12, you see the center figure as 13. But if you're reading across the line, you see it as the letter B. It has to do with the context of your perspective. And a seven-year-old boy or a fifteen-year-old girl is bound to have a different perspective from Mom's or Dad's. Parents who don't practice empathy never seem to get that.

> ## IF THE CONVERSATION STALLS
> Resist the urge to press your tween or teen about details of the day or his or her friends. Forcing a conversation at this stage is typically unproductive. Let it unfold on its own. If it doesn't happen routinely, that's okay. In time, the information will come.

WHAT IF MY CHILD WON'T TALK?

That's not an unusual question. Some kids can sit through an entire meal and never open up—unless their parents know the secret of empathy.

The truth is that 70 to 80 percent of all communication is nonverbal. So in reality you can't *not* communicate. If you're sincere in your desire to understand, you won't just be listening for words, you'll be reading body language and facial expressions. You'll sense the spirit and mood of your child—even when he or she is silent. Empathy helps you to pick up on what's being said when nothing is being said.

Some well-intentioned parents make the mistake of probing: "Don't you feel well?" "Is something wrong?" "Do you want to talk about it?" Try this, and the likely response will be further withdrawal.

On the other hand, when you gently say something like, "I'm wondering if you didn't have a very good day at school," you're not probing. Your comment isn't threatening. But it does let your child know you're present and mindful—and ready to listen when he or she talks. All this is predicated on having an empathetic heart that's sincere, flexible, and humble.

HOW TO WALK IN YOUR KIDS' SNEAKERS

- ♦ Set aside your own agenda temporarily to focus your attention on your children.
- ♦ Turn on your emotional radar to discover what they are feeling under the surface.
- ♦ Use your head and heart to think and feel your way into their perspective. (This can take time, so be patient.)

IT'S QUICKER THAN YOU THINK

In *Winning with People,* John Maxwell recounts the following story, which demonstrates the benefit and importance of seeing an issue from the other person's perspective:

> In the 1930s, American Airways, which later became American Airlines, had a tremendous problem with complaints from passengers about lost luggage. LaMotte Cohn, general manager of the airline at the time, tried to get his station managers to overcome this issue, but he saw little progress. Finally he came up with an idea to help the airline's personnel to see things from their customers' points of view. Cohn asked all of the station managers from across the country to fly to company headquarters for a meeting. Then he made sure that every manager's luggage was

lost in transit. Afterward, the airline suddenly made a huge leap of efficiency in that area.[7]

Did you see that one coming? The situation quickly and dramatically improved, and all because the airline's station managers instantly saw the problem from their customers' points of view.

When you accurately see any situation from your children's point of view, when you can experience it like they do, you instantly take a different approach to the situation, and a great connection is the result. We know that the word *instantly* carries a strong promise, but it's accurate. Should we soften it by saying "almost instantly"? We don't think so. Empathy can actually change everything in a moment. As soon as you see a predicament from your children's angles, once you have put yourself in their shoes, you change—that very instant. You have more grace, more understanding. You have the heart of great table talk. That's the promise of fast-acting empathy.

FROM STEPHANIE
We love the Disney movie *Ratatouille*! Our kids (and we adults) watched it over and over again. What a great inspiration to get kids cooking with adults. Make the dinner on the following page, then eat it and watch the movie—together.

Ratatouille Fondue (serves 6 to 8)

1 cup sliced mushrooms

1 cup diced yellow onion

8-ounce jar of roasted red bell peppers, drained and chopped

½ cup sliced black olives

1 cup chopped artichoke hearts

2 cups chopped precooked chicken sausages (we like the spicy ones)

1 cup canned diced tomatoes, with juice

2 teaspoons chopped garlic

1 teaspoon kosher salt

1 teaspoon pepper

¼ cup olive oil

1 cup shredded Parmesan cheese

1 cup nonfat sour cream

1 cup chicken broth

Mix all ingredients and seal in an airtight container. Refrigerate overnight or freeze. When you're ready to use, thaw completely if frozen, and cook in a slow cooker on low for 6 to 8 hours. You can also simmer the thawed mixture on the stove top in a large pot over medium-low heat for 3 to 4 hours, stirring often, or cook in a covered Dutch oven in a 325° oven for 2 to 3 hours, stirring once every hour.

Serve warm with sourdough bread or as an appetizer with pita chips.

5 | How to Listen So Your Kids Talk

The first duty of love is to listen.

PAUL TILLICH

"HEY, PAL, how was your day?"

"Fine."

"Did you do anything interesting at school?"

"Not really."

"How about spaghetti for dinner tonight?"

"I guess."

If you have a child older than ten, you've no doubt experienced this conversation, or something like it, before. Almost every parent has. So the question begging to be answered is, how can I have quality conversations that consistently engage my child?

Countless books have been written on the subject. An endless array of parenting seminars have talked about the issue. And what do they all say? For one thing, nearly every expert agrees that quality conversations begin with caring. To paraphrase an old adage, your kids don't care how much you know until they know how much you care.

Have you ever given this much thought? Don't feel guilty if you haven't. Most of us haven't. Caring is so essential to a good conversation that it often goes unnoticed. If you ask parents to list the ingredients of good communication, you'll find that caring generally doesn't even make the list. How do we know? We've surveyed hundreds of parents with that very question. But consider this: once you take caring out of a conversation, your kids will stop talking. When caring is gone, the conversation is over. Enough said.

So if you want to enjoy fantastic conversations around your dinner table, you've got to listen so your kids will talk. With that in mind, let's review a little "Communication 101."[1]

LISTENING IS NOT HEARING

If you can hear, you can listen—right? Wrong. Hearing is passive. *Listening is active.*

A sage once said that the Lord gave us two ears and one mouth, and that ratio ought to tell us something. It's a good point. And to drive the point home further, in 1948, American psychologist Theodor Reik, one of Sigmund Freud's earliest and most brilliant students, wrote a book called *Listening with the Third Ear*. The book was his way of underscoring the fact that listening is not about hearing words. It's about hearing the message *behind* the words.

TWO MAJOR INGREDIENTS OF ACTIVE LISTENING

Two major ingredients go into active listening: clarification and reflection. Let's take a look at each of these.

1 *Clarification*
First, active listening requires clarification. How do
you read the two lines below?

Love
isnowhere.

Some see "Love is nowhere." Others see "Love is now here."
In the same way, what seems clear to us as parents may
have an entirely different meaning from the one our children actually receive. That's why clarification is essential
to good listening. Clarification serves two basic purposes:
(1) it gathers additional information, and (2) it helps
explore an issue more thoroughly. Of course, clarification
is also necessary when we are not sure *we* heard correctly.

Misunderstandings do not result from not hearing the
words but from our not *clarifying* the content. Did you
know that for the words in the English language we most
commonly use, there are more than fourteen hundred different meanings?

So whether we're communicating with teenagers or
toddlers, clarification is essential to good listening. One of
the easiest ways to practice clarification with an older child
is to use that tried-and-true response, "What I hear you
saying is . . ." But you can also ask something like, "Can you
tell me a little more to make sure I understand?" Or ask a
more specific question:

Child: "I guess we were supposed to turn in a page or
something."
You: "You had an assignment you didn't finish on time?"

To recap, when we clarify, we're gathering additional information or exploring an issue more thoroughly.

2 Reflection

Second, active listening requires *reflection*. Active listening does not mean saying, "I understand." A classic cartoon shows an exasperated teenager telling her mother, "For Pete's sake, will you stop understanding me and just listen?"

At issue here is preconception; that is, the listener has a *preconceived* idea of what the speaker means. "I'm not going to do my homework" may actually mean "I was terribly embarrassed by Mr. Wilson for reading my assignment to the whole class." "I won't go" may mean "I don't want to go." And the parents who learn how to reflect their child's feelings discover the difference.

The goal is to target one of three aspects of a message in your reflections: (1) the content of the message, (2) the thinking behind the message, and (3) the feeling behind the message. Each is equally valid and useful. Here is an example of how a single statement may be reflected at each level.

Child: "I couldn't believe he was accusing me of doing what *he* did."

Parent (reflecting the meaning of the statement): "He blamed you."

Child (feeling understood): "Yeah. He said I was the one responsible because I was there."

Parent (reflecting what the child is thinking): "You thought he was unfair."

Child (feeling understood): "Yeah. I didn't deserve to be blamed."

Parent (reflecting child's feeling): "That must have made you angry."

Child (feeling emotionally safe in speaking honestly): "I was furious. I also felt bad."[2]

Did you notice that the parent in this scenario didn't ask a single question? It was all about reflection. And each time the parent did so, the child opened up all the more. By the way, if you think this is just some manufactured illustration that doesn't work in real life, we have a challenge for you. Sometime in the next twenty-four hours, we want you to give this a try. When your child brings up a topic of conversation, do nothing more than reflect your child's statements, thinking, and feeling. We think you'll be amazed at just how remarkably powerful this simple strategy works.

Why does this time-tested approach work so well? Because whenever we simply reflect someone else's meaning, we are not evaluating or advising. We are saying, "I am with you and want to understand you better."

PANNING FOR GOLD

Every child is a unique book for parents. We can't assume we know what our kids are feeling if we haven't studied them carefully. When we listen to our children with the "third ear," it's similar to panning for gold. Just as a miner sifts through sand and pebbles to find a golden nugget, our jobs as attentive parents are to sift through our children's communication (including nonverbal clues) and lift out the nuggets of emotion, hold them carefully, then hand them back to our children saying, "Here, is this how you feel?"

To be in your children's memories tomorrow, you have to be in their lives today.

ANONYMOUS

We can't overstate the value of mastering the skill of listening for your children's feelings. Few things will open their hearts to you more. Few things will endear you to your children more. When you listen with the third ear, you not only hear the emotions they aren't talking about but also help them put those emotions into words. Here's an example of this at work in the life of Justin, a thirteen-year-old who refuses to do his homework:

Justin: "I don't care what you or the school wants to do to me. I'm not going to do another assignment for that teacher."

Mom (restraining her desire to lay down the law): "Sounds as if you've made up your mind."

Justin: "Yep. Mr. Wilson is an idiot. They shouldn't even allow him to be at that school."

Mom: "He's not too smart, huh?"

Justin: "Well, I'm sure he's smart and everything, but he isn't very nice."

Mom: "He's treated you kind of mean?"

Justin: "Yeah. The last time I handed in my paper, Wilson read it out loud. I didn't write it for the whole world to hear."

Mom: "You felt betrayed."

Justin: "Exactly! What would you do if you were me?"[3]

Can you put yourself in this mother's place? Consider the restraint that you, as a parent, need to have to muster up this kind of empathy and really listen for your child's feelings. But also notice the reward that results from attentive listening. Once you've displayed a caring attitude and accurately identified your children's emotions, their spirits open up almost instantaneously.

ACTIVE LISTENING DOES THREE THINGS

We've looked at what active listening requires on the part of parents. Now we want to turn our attention to the results of active listening. All three outcomes help to improve communication and contribute to making a home the safest place there is. Let's look at each one.

1. Active Listening Unearths Hidden Feelings

Almost all parents sometimes feel that their children—especially as they enter the teen years—are burying their feelings. But active listening unearths them. How? By allowing their children's emotions to emerge, especially when the children want someone to *sense* their feelings without having to reveal them. This sounds unfair, if not a bit crazy, we know. But truth be told, the cry of fear sometimes hides behind a fuming face. And pain is sometimes disguised as wordy anger.

2. Active Listening Takes Away the Fear of Feeling

You probably know the feeling of sinking into a big leather easy chair. *Ahh.* You can just relax. Put your feet up. That's similar to the feeling our child has when your active listening creates an emotionally safe place, free from evaluation. You'll see that this is where kids begin to shed their defenses—and sense that their emotions are acceptable and even appreciated. Kids can relax in your presence.

3. Active Listening Helps Kids Solve Their Problems

One of the most common mistakes we make in trying to help our children is to be too quick with offering advice. Like a gunslinger in the old West, we like to fire off solutions and defeat our children's problems before we even know what they are. And like all of us, kids don't appreciate trigger-happy problem solvers or advice givers. Not only that, but if we make a habit of prematurely solving problems for our children, they never learn to be resourceful themselves. In fact, they become overly dependent. Why? Because giving too much advice too frequently can communicate, "I don't trust you to come up with your own solution." But active listening says, "I believe in you and know you are a resourceful person."

CLARIFY BEFORE YOU CONDEMN

Have you ever had a child refuse to do something you wanted? Kind of a dumb question, right? Recently our little Jackson refused to take a vitamin we'd set on his dinner plate. "I don't want to take this vitamin!" he wailed. Our first instinct was to exercise our "parental authority" and force the issue by making him take it anyway. Instead, we asked a simple question, the answer to which seemed painfully obvious: "You don't want to take your vitamin today?"

But Jackson's answer surprised us. "No, I don't want *this* one," he said. "I want my Scooby-Doo vitamin."

Well, that was easy. Problem solved. We could have spent a torturous meal together by forcing Jackson to take his vitamin—all because we thought he was being defiant. Instead, we simply heard him out and discovered his real issue. That was that.

This kind of listening becomes even more important to our relationships with our children when they become teens. If you sincerely and continually uncover what your child values—whether it be a particular video game, a certain brand of perfume, or a type of music—as a way to understand your child's heart, you'll have a direct line to his or her world.

> # The most important thing in communication is to hear what isn't being said.
>
> PETER F. DRUCKER

This simple strategy of clarifying before you reflexively condemn will save you untold moments of anguish. And although a teenager's values will sometimes surprise you, remember that if you don't know about them you don't stand a chance of influencing them. So listen attentively, of course. But don't forget to restrain your knee-jerk judgment until your child is sure you fully understand.

LISTEN AS IF YOU MEAN IT

This is something few parents understand. Whenever you carefully listen to your children, reflecting their experience, you're subconsciously telling them that they're important to you. It doesn't matter their age. When children know you are invested in understanding them, when you're giving them your undivided attention when they speak, you're doing nothing less than encouraging their very souls. Think about it. Where else are they lavished with this kind of attention?

It's easier than you think. Simply look your children in the eye when they are talking to you (being careful not to stare them down). That's where it starts. In addition, you need to set aside whatever you're doing—including your cell phone. If the children are toddlers, you might even get down on one knee from time to time so you can listen to them at their eye level. Whatever your children's age or stage, you can always listen as if you mean it. And they'll love you for it.

DOUGHNUT DATES

That's what my mom and I (Leslie) called the times we had together, starting when I was in the sixth grade. Mom initiated this standing appointment with me each week, and we'd meet at the neighborhood doughnut shop. It wasn't fancy, of course. It was fun. Almost every week—until I left home for college—we met with no agenda other than to connect. We didn't study a book together. Nothing was planned. It was merely a consistent time to get together, just the two of us. What did we talk about? Anything and everything. And more often than not, it usually involved relationships. Did Mom give advice? Rarely. Mom didn't jump in to solve problems or give unsolicited advice. She just listened.

Only now, as I write these words, do I really realize what an amazing gift these times with my mom were. She was a busy pastor's wife, but I know she made our dough-nut date a top priority even though she had plenty of other activities that could have crowded it out. To this day our connection runs deep. And on occasion, we still meet at a local doughnut shop.[4]

MAD, SAD, GLAD

We make listening a daily ritual at our house. With two young boys we decided we needed a routine to help us stay in tune with one another. That's where the exercise we call "Mad, Sad, and Glad" comes in. We're not rigid about it, but nearly every day, at some point—over dinner, while stuck in traffic, or at bedtime—we'll say, "Let's do Mad, Sad, and Glad." It has become such a habit, in fact, that often our boys will initiate it. First, each of us takes a moment to tell everyone else about one thing that made us mad that day. John, for example, might say, "I got kind of mad when Jacob didn't really let me do my part of our shared presentation in class." We listen and ask a follow-up question or two. Then we tell about one thing that made us sad. John might say, "I really wanted to check out a library book that Jordan got before me, and that made me a little sad." Again we listen and interact with him. Finally, we share one thing that made us glad. John might say, "I was really glad that we got to go swimming at Grandmother's today."

Of course, each of us takes a turn. And as the boys have gotten older, it's been fun to see them ask us follow-up questions about what made us mad, sad, or glad. This little ritual is amazingly simple, but it works wonders for getting children of all ages to open up. In fact, it can become the centerpiece of an entire dinner conversation if family members learn to ask good questions.[5]

THE ART OF THE OPEN-ENDED QUESTION

A rookie mistake for any parent wanting to generate a good conversation around the dinner table is to ask questions that go nowhere. For example: "Did you have a good day at school?" Fair enough. Sounds solid. But it's likely to get a short answer because it's a closed question requiring a mere yes or no.

"What happened today at school?" on the other hand, opens up a conversation. You can't answer that with a yes or no. It elicits detailed information. Here are some examples of open-ended questions:

- "What were you most proud of today at school?"
- "What can you tell me about your new teacher?"
- "Why do you think your coach has you do so many laps?"
- "How did you end up solving that problem with your friend?"

HOW TO READ YOUR KID'S MIND

Here's a little exercise called "Let Me Read Your Mind." It can help you improve your listening efforts immediately.

If you have a child about six years of age or older and you're wondering what's really going on inside her head, say, "I'd like to read your mind." She'll love it. Then tell her what it is you are hearing her say or what you sense she is thinking. Here's an example:

You: "I'd like to read your mind."

Child: "Okay."

You: "Just before dinner tonight when I was helping you with your homework, you got your feelings hurt because I was in a hurry. Am I right?"

Now your child simply rates how accurate (or inaccurate) you are on a scale of 1 to 10, 10 being right on the money.

Child: "That's about a 3. I could tell you were in a hurry but it didn't really bother me."

Of course, it's only fair to let your child read your mind as well:

Child: "I'd like to read your mind."

You: "Okay."

Child: "I think you're upset because I didn't finish my project for Scouts without you telling me to yesterday."

You: "Well, you're right. That's about a 7 or maybe even an 8. I know you have a major milestone with your troop next week, and I don't like to be the one who has to remind you to get what you need to do to earn your next badge."

Do you get the idea? This little exercise cuts through a lot of misunderstanding. It allows your children to put their fears and frustrations on the table, without receiving condemnation, to see if they're valid.

You may be thinking that you will try this exercise of "mind reading" sometime. If you really want to put it into practice, try it tonight over dinner. Explain how it works and go for it. You'll soon see exactly how easy it is to do.[6]

LISTEN SLOWLY

Pastor Chuck Swindoll tells of a day when he learned an important lesson about listening:

> *I vividly remember some time back being caught in the undertow of too many commitments in too few days. It wasn't long before I was snapping at my wife and our children, choking down my food at mealtimes, and feeling irritated at those unexpected interruptions through the day. Before long, things around our home began reflecting the pattern of my hurry-up style. It was becoming unbearable. I distinctly recall after supper one evening the words of our younger daughter Colleen. She wanted to tell me about something important that had happened to her at school that day. She hurriedly began, "Daddy, I wanna tell you somethin' andI willtellyoureallyfast."*
>
> *Suddenly realizing her frustration, I answered, "Honey, you can tell me . . . and you don't have to tell me really fast. Say it slowly."*
>
> *I'll never forget her answer: "Then listen slowly."*[7]

How would you listen if your son were suddenly a national hero or your boss? How would you listen if your daughter came down from Mars or had the future of the world stored in her mind or knew the cure for cancer? Thinking in these terms may sound silly, but it's a proven technique for creating mindfulness and giving your full attention to your child—even if the topic of conversation is the four-square game at recess.

That about says it, doesn't it? *Listen slowly.* Who couldn't benefit from that advice? We offer our children a tremendous gift when we take a moment to listen not only to their words but to the feelings behind the words.

TRY SLOW COOKING

Slow cookers are wonderful tools to help you get a home-cooked dinner on your table because dinner can be ready to serve when you get home! Tina's recipe for BBQ Short Ribs works well in a slow cooker, as do many recipes for roasts, chicken, soups, and stews.

FROM TINA

Our family cabin on the lake is a refuge from our busy life. It's the perfect getaway, about an hour from home, semi-rustic, with no cell-phone service! You never quite know who will show up on a sunny afternoon or how long they will stay, and everyone is hungry after playing on the lake. On the next page we have included a wonderful recipe we start in the morning and let simmer all day. We all get to enjoy our day, and no one gets stuck in the kitchen for hours.

Slow-Cooked BBQ Short Ribs

3 pounds boneless country-style beef short ribs
½ chopped onion
2 tablespoons oil

In a heavy skillet over high heat, add oil, onions, and ribs, browning
ribs by cooking 2 to 3 minutes per side.

Combine sauce ingredients in slow cooker:
¼ cup vinegar
2 tablespoons sugar
½ cup ketchup
½ cup barbecue sauce (your favorite brand)
3 tablespoons Worcestershire sauce
1 teaspoon dry mustard
2 teaspoons salt

Add browned ribs and onion to slow cooker. Cook 6 to 8 hours
(depending on your slow cooker). If you are pinched for time and/or
do not have all the sauce ingredients, you can combine raw short
ribs and an entire bottle of barbecue
sauce in the slow cooker and cook.

6 | Curbing Conflict at the Table and Beyond

*Better a dry crust eaten in peace than a house
filled with feasting—and conflict.*

PROVERBS 17:1

WE WERE GATHERED around our family table for tacos, the oversize lazy Susan loaded with mounds of simple, fresh ingredients to layer into our warmed shells. Jackson spoke up as he spun the tray around to make sure the cheese was all the way across the table by his brother, John, and as far away from him as possible.

"Yuck! I hate cheese," he said, as he loaded his shell with spicy taco meat.

Meanwhile John was loading his shell with almost nothing but cheese when I prompted him, "Be sure to add some beans or meat, please."

John pointed to his brother and said, "That's not fair. If I have to eat beans, you have to make Jack eat cheese."

"No way!" said Jackson, expressing his feelings loud and clear with a distorted face. "Cheese is the worst!"

Just another meal at the Parrott dinner table? Pretty much. It seems that opportunities for tension and conflict are never far away.

Of course, the issue isn't always between siblings. Sometimes parents unwittingly get sucked in to the mix. Take the Brinley family, for example. Matthew, a usually ravenous teenager, sits down at the dinner table, but his mom notices that he is barely touching the chicken.

"Don't you like the chicken, Matt?"

"Um, sure . . ."

"Why aren't you eating it?"

"Well, because it's white meat, and I like dark meat."

His younger brother, slyly holding up a drumstick, says, "Like this?"

"Whatever," Matthew says as he rolls his eyes.

Mom launches into a soliloquy on the price of chicken, making it clear that she's not running a restaurant so Matt needs to eat what she serves.

"It's okay, Mom," interrupts Matthew. "I'm eating the potatoes. I'm fine."

"Honey," his mom continues, "why don't you eat the white meat just for once? You're getting too picky when it comes to food. When I was your age . . ."

Matthew tunes out the rest of her story because he suddenly recalls a statement he heard her make while she was talking on the phone a few days ago. His parents had just returned from looking at samples of new kitchen cabinets at a showroom, and his mother was recounting the experience to a good friend.

"There were so many different styles and different

~
**Mama's
Macaroni
and Cheese,**
page 14
~

~
**Super Simple
Sloppy Joes,**
page 30
~

~
**Hearty Garden
Patch Soup,** *page 46*
~

~ **Ratatouille Fondue,** *page 60* ~

~

**Slow-Cooked
BBQ Short Ribs,**
page 76

~

~ **Grilled Raspberry Chicken,** *page 93* ~

Chicken Fajitas,
page 105

Smoky Sausage and Cheddar Potatoes, *page 127*

Zesty Lemon Pork Chops,
page 144

**Tomato Bacon
Egg Strata,**
page 157

**Asian Chopped
Chicken Salad,**
page 166

Spanish Eggs,
page 171

shades of wood to choose from," she had said. "I just couldn't make up my mind. My husband got really impatient and said I was too picky. I told him that I wasn't being picky; I was merely making a 'preference analysis.'"

Now, back to the dinner table and the chicken issue, Matthew asks, "Am I being 'picky' or am I just making a 'preference analysis'?"

"What are you talking about?" his mom asks.

Matt reminds her of the cabinet conversation he overheard on the phone and says, "What's the difference between being choosy with your food and being choosy over your cabinets?"

Teenagers are masters at spotting inconsistencies. For Matthew, this is a glaring example.

And that is the moment his mom gets sucked in. "They are completely different! Do you know how hard I worked to put this food together for you tonight?" With that the conversation gets kicked into high gear and eventually ends with Matthew leaving the table, storming off, and slamming the door to his bedroom.

It's not at all what Mom had in mind when she was preparing the food. But it's what happens at far too many dinner tables. Of course, conflict doesn't require parents— or even teenagers. Your little darlings can simultaneously shriek "Mine!" as they rip a coloring book in two. Conflict ensues long before they come to the table.

That's why in this chapter we're offering practical and proven helps for curbing conflict at the dinner table and beyond.

THE HOUR THAT MATTERS MOST

WHAT ARE WE FIGHTING ABOUT?

Let's say you have two children, ages three and eight. And let's say they are typical. They argue in the backseat of the car because one of them wants "quiet time" while the other wants music. They argue about the seating arrangement for dinner (who gets the special wooden chair or who gets to sit next to which parent). They argue about one being in the other's physical space ("Stop touching me!") and over toys ("I had that first!"). Unfortunately, the arguing doesn't end as children get older. They argue with you about the clothes they want to wear. The food you serve. The color of their bedroom walls. Where they go and how they get there. The people they hang with. What time they go to bed. Nearly anything can make the fur fly in most families. But here's what researchers say are the top six points of contention among family members:

> Lord, when we are wrong, make us willing to change. And when we are right, make us easy to live with.
>
> PETER MARSHALL

1. Sharing possessions
2. Who started the argument
3. Which TV shows to watch
4. Siblings in another's room or space
5. Chores
6. Food

CHOOSING YOUR BATTLES

One of the first words of wisdom experts pass along to new parents is to choose their battles wisely.

You've probably seen the "Grant me the wisdom to accept the things I cannot change" prayer on plaques and posters. It may be overfamiliar, but it's true: one of the major tasks of parenting is learning what can and should be changed (talking back or showing disrespect, for example) and what should be overlooked (accidentally spilling a glass of milk).

We often tell parents that the majority of the issues they bicker about with their kids can probably be overlooked. We know how easy it is to condemn and criticize when we want our kids to behave well. We end up yapping about minor infractions that turn into major squabbles. As parents it's easy and natural to sweat the small stuff. But following this simple advice about choosing your battles can keep you from ruining a family meal or even an entire vacation. So before you gripe about the way your children made their beds or cleared the table, ask yourself whether it's worth it.

LOWER DEFENSES TO LOWER THE TENSION

Conflict always escalates when someone gets defensive. No matter our age, we all know how to put on an emotional suit of armor and dig in our heels. And as soon as we do, reasoning goes out the window and irrational thinking and behavior settle in.

You can keep defensiveness at bay, however, by using a simple technique we've used in marriage counseling—but it works with kids, too. We call it the "X, Y, Z formula."

Think of this approach as a kind of game in which you fill in the blanks with your particular gripe in mind: "In situation X, when you do Y, I feel Z." For example, "When you come home from school (X) and throw your coat on the floor (Y), I feel like you think of me as your maid instead of your mom (Z)." That's very different from saying, "You never hang up your coat!"

Or, "When I'm trying to talk with you (X) and you walk away from me without saying anything (Y), I feel confused and even a little upset (Z)." That's likely to be received far better than, "You'd better show me some respect when I'm talking to you!"

Using this formula will help you avoid insults and putdowns and, instead, allow you to simply state how your children's behavior affects your feelings. And when they get a glimpse into your feelings, they will have more empathy for you—and maybe less conflict with you. In short, the X, Y, Z formula helps your child receive a message without getting defensive.

IDENTIFY CONFLICT TRIGGERS

Here's something that everyone—including you—can benefit from. And it's a simple exercise you can do together as a family around the table. Each person finishes the following half-dozen sentences:

1. Most of my conflicts at home are with _____ _____.

2. They usually happen because _____ _____.

3. What bothers me most is when this person ____

   _____.

4. When this person does this, I usually feel _____

   _____.

5. And here's what I usually do: _____

   _____.

6. The next time a conflict with this person happens,
   I can make it better by _____.

Of course, to make this exercise effective, you need to do it when everyone is getting along. In other words, don't try it if a conflict is already brewing. As each person shares, keep a nonjudgmental attitude. As you and your family identify what triggers conflict for each person, you'll give that trigger less power.

NO YELLING ALLOWED

It's a good idea to have some family rules in place before a conflict heats up. Here's one that is sure to help: no yelling allowed. This requires everyone to use a relatively calm voice. It doesn't mean family members can't get emotional. But a person who loses the ability to speak calmly must leave the table until he or she calms down. Again, this is a rule to agree upon before the next conflict breaks out.

EATING HUMBLE PIE

I (Leslie) had just walked into the kitchen to find Jackson, then two, with this clothes completely soaked with milk. "Why did you do that, John?" I snapped. Our seven-year-old had tried to give his little brother a drink and evidently was careless. John started to answer, but I interrupted. "Jackson can't drink this kind of milk, and look at the mess you've made!"

But as I was changing Jackson's clothes, it suddenly dawned on me. John had been trying to help. He'd simply been trying to give his little brother some milk. But because I'd impulsively scolded John, I knew I needed to apologize. "I'm sorry, John," I told him. "I shouldn't have spoken so harshly to you when you were being so nice to share your milk with Jack." John's look of relief said it all. I'd done the right thing.

No matter how much we love our children, we still make mistakes, misjudge situations and motives, and sometimes lose our tempers. That's why we all need an occasional slice of humble pie.

Whatever your child's age, an honest apology won't automatically undo the damage, of course. But it will almost always restore your relationship with your child and keep conflict at bay.[1]

"It is so important for an adult to apologize, because it shows the child it's okay to make mistakes and say you are

Try This

If you're having trouble getting everyone to the table on time, set up a known consequence for the dawdlers. Whoever is last to the table becomes the server, pouring the drinks, fetching anything that's needed, and so on. But there's a catch: even if the first to arrive hasn't washed his or her hands, this child ends up serving— with clean hands, of course!

sorry," says Dr. John Gottman. "When you say, 'I shouldn't have done that,' your child will have a rock-solid sense that her feelings matter to the people who are most important in her life."[2]

A LITTLE RESPECT GOES A LONG WAY

If you want to reduce conflict with your kids, a proven strategy is to show them respect. Here are some of the most common ways to show your children respect:

* Knock before entering your children's rooms, especially if their doors are closed.
* When someone asks your children a question, let them answer for themselves. Resist the temptation to speak for your children, especially when they are present.
* Value your children's need for fun and the time they spend with friends.
* Value your children's need for privacy. Don't open their mail or listen in on their phone conversations.
* Give your children space to have opinions and preferences that are different from yours.
* If your children are struggling with something and are in no danger of getting hurt, hurting someone else, or ruining anything valuable, ask them if they want help before you step in and fix the problem.

CRITICISM VERSUS COMPLAINING

Have you ever been inspired with an idea while taking a shower? That's what happened to Rev. Will Bowen. He became weary of hearing parishioners at his Kansas City church complain about everything from the choice of hymns at the Sunday service to the informal dress code at the church's Saturday night worship. So he asked his flock to take a pledge not to complain, criticize, gossip, or use sarcasm for twenty-one days. The concept has spread, and people who join the cause are issued little purple bracelets as a reminder of their pledge to quit complaining. If they catch themselves complaining, they're supposed to take off the bracelet, switch it to the opposite wrist, and start counting the days from scratch.[3]

That sounds like a pretty good idea, doesn't it? After all, wouldn't you like to eliminate complaining from your family? Interestingly, though, some research has shown that moderate complaining helps us air our grievances and keep improving. In moderation, it can actually be good for relationships. What isn't helpful to our relationships is criticism.

> Live so that when your children think of fairness and integrity, they think of you.
>
> H. JACKSON BROWN JR.

What's the difference between criticism and complaining? Criticism almost always begins with *you*. ("You always make food I don't like!") Complaining almost always begins with *I*. ("I'm disappointed that we're having green beans again.") This may seem like a small matter of semantics, but it makes a big difference around the dinner table and beyond.

Of course, this can be a tall order for a little one who is refusing to eat, but if you institute a "no criticism rule" at the table while allowing your young ones to "complain" a bit, you'll likely see their jaws drop, and then you'll see a reduction in tension. All that's required is a clear explanation of the difference between criticism and complaining along with—and this is the tough part—good modeling from Mom and Dad. After all, you can't expect your kids to follow the rule if you don't. But when you're doing this as a family, you can make it fun. Soon, your kids will be policing your critical comments, so beware.

RATE THE INTENSITY OF YOUR FEELINGS

Very few people enjoy conflict. And when it rears its head at the dinner table, the meal ends up ruined for everyone. But we have a proven technique for managing conflict. For several years now, we have been handing out hundreds of what we call "Conflict Cards" (you can download one for free at our website: www.RealRelationships.com). Using this small card helps put people on even ground when it comes to expressing the intensity of their feelings. We are not sure where the idea for this card came from, but it has helped us resolve plenty of conflicts in our own marriage and now with our kids. And we've seen it work for countless other families.

The idea is simple. On the card is a scale from one to ten ranking the intensity of a person's feelings:

1. I'm not enthusiastic, but it's no big deal to me.
2. I don't see it the way you do, but I may be wrong.

3. I don't agree, but I can live with it.
4. I don't agree, but I'll let you have your way.
5. I don't agree and cannot remain silent on this.
6. I do not approve, and I need more time.
7. I strongly disapprove and cannot go along with it.
8. I will be so seriously upset I can't predict my reaction.
9. No possible way! If you do, I quit!
10. Over my dead body!

Anytime a heated exchange occurs, you can simply pull this list out and rank the level of disagreement. ("This is a three for me." "It's a five for me.") With our kids, we typically have them write down their rankings, and then we share them. By rating their conflict, they can play on a level field even when one person is more expressive than the other. It doesn't work for every family, but it's worth a try.[4]

REVIST THE AMAZING POWER OF EMPATHY

We talked in chapter 4 about empathy as the heart of great table talk. Some people say empathy is inefficient, that it takes too much time and effort when it comes to curbing

> **TINA'S TIP**
> When our kids don't want to eat what I've cooked for dinner, we don't make an issue of it. Instead, they don't have to eat it as long as they've tried at least one bite, which we call the "no thank you" bite. If they refuse to eat even that bite, however, they must wait to eat anything more until the next meal. This system keeps me from being a short-order cook, and it gets the kids to try new foods.

Try This

If you have children who make a habit out of tilting their chairs back on two legs, you can almost instantly break the habit by having them stand up to eat for five minutes. Do this tongue-in-cheek and talk about how tough it is to break unhealthy habits. Of course, if the kids catch you tilting your chair back, be prepared for the same consequence.

conflict. We couldn't disagree more. Empathy is highly pragmatic. It saves untold time in moving past difficulties, and it accelerates connection.

Think of any convoluted conversation you've ever had with a child. Maybe it was a misunderstanding about a homework assignment or involved misread motivations concerning a comment. Maybe a lack of appreciation after you had slaved away in the kitchen caused you to clam up. Whatever the issue, wouldn't you like a way to make the conflict immediately disappear? Wouldn't you like a magic button that would suddenly make things better and get everyone back on the same team? Well, that's what putting yourself in your child's shoes can do.

For example, we recently had a conversation with our thirteen-year-old, just before dinner, that became increasingly heated. It involved a party we were hosting in our home.

"I don't want enchiladas," John asserted. "I hate them."

"Honey, you've always liked enchiladas," I (Leslie) replied.

"Well, I don't anymore," John shouted and started to leave the room.

"Where are you going?" I asked.

"I'm putting the ice cream in the freezer like you asked me to," he hollered back.

I followed him into the kitchen, and he could feel me gearing up for a hardheaded discourse on why enchiladas were great for the party and how he needed to think of the guests, not just himself.

But before we made it to the softening ice cream, I turned to him, put my hands on his shoulders, and said, "Help me see this from your side."

That's all it took. In less than a minute he told me the last time we had enchiladas he got a tummy ache. But something about the way he said it made me think that wasn't the real story.

"So is that the reason you don't want me to make enchiladas?"

"Well, that, and I know Michael doesn't like them. He said so at lunch just yesterday."

Ah. Now we were getting to it. John didn't want to have a dish that disappointed a good friend. Why he didn't say that at the start, only a kid's brain knows. But when he sensed that I genuinely wanted to see the issue from his perspective, John's heart softened toward me.

"That makes sense," I said. "We should have something you think everyone will enjoy."

That was it. In a moment's time, I caught a glimpse of his world from his perspective, and the tension melted long before the ice cream on the kitchen counter did.

The point is that without a bit of empathy, our enchilada exchange would have likely dragged on and evolved into an emotional and a time-consuming upheaval that neither of us wanted.

You get the point. So, don't let anyone tell you empathy is time consuming. It's not. Nothing dispels tension faster than empathy.

CONVERSATION STARTERS

- When are you most likely to lose your temper, and why?
- Name three pet peeves that drive you crazy.
- If you were the parent in this family, what would you do differently?
- What do you think starts most arguments?
- What is one thing you can do to try to calm down when you feel frustrated?

STEER CLEAR OF PUT-DOWNS

In spite of the good intentions of the old childhood rhyme about how "sticks and stones" are different from "words" because sticks and stones can cause physical pain, we all know the truth. Words do hurt. They may not break our bones, but they can surely break our spirits. Tune in to a few choice words uttered without a thought in many homes: "You're so selfish." "You are so unkind." "You're like a little pig."

Put-downs like these are lethal, and one of the sad facts of close family relationships is that we treat the ones we love worse than we treat just about anyone else. Research has shown that it takes only one put-down to undo hours of kindness. So why not make a family pact to avoid put-downs altogether?

CONFLICT BUSTER

The following is from a great friend and employee of ours who has four children, nine to fourteen years old at the time she gave the suggestion to me. This is what they do in their home to eliminate their dinnertime conflicts: "One of the things we do as a way of resolving conflict is to take turns being the 'server.' One child a week gets to be the server for a day. That person basically waits on everyone else—takes their orders, brings them napkins, refills drinks, and so on. It forces everyone to use good manners, and it is pretty hard to fight with someone who is bringing you an extra chocolate milk."

FROM TINA

When we were kids, my grandmother made wonderful fried chicken. I really wanted to make old-fashioned fried chicken for my family, but I did not want to make something so high in fat. I found this healthier alternative, and everyone loves it. My sister and I made it every time we got together for our fix-and-freeze assembly day.

Grilled Raspberry Chicken (serves 6)

Place 1 resealable bag of 8 chicken pieces (2 breasts, 2 thighs, and 4 legs) inside a stable container and fold edges of bag over. Add the following:

¼ teaspoon black pepper
¼ teaspoon crushed red pepper
1 teaspoon chopped garlic
1 tablespoon ginger puree
½ cup raspberry preserves
2 tablespoons rice wine vinegar
2 tablespoons orange juice concentrate
½ cup hoisin sauce

Place sealed bag of chicken and marinade in a wide pan and cover with a lid. Affix cooking instructions to lid.

Cooking Instructions

1. Thaw in refrigerator, if frozen.
2. Remove chicken from marinade (reserve marinade for glaze). Place chicken pieces in baking pan sprayed with nonstick cooking spray.
3. Place baking pan on grill; cook in covered grill on medium-high for 30 to 35 minutes, or bake in a conventional oven at 375° for 30 to 35 minutes (or until internal temperature reaches 165°).
4. Meanwhile, bring marinade to a boil, reduce heat, and simmer 10 to 15 minutes until thickened into a glaze (internal temperature 140°). If it becomes too thick, stir in a little hot water.
5. Baste chicken with glaze halfway through cooking.

Serve remaining glaze on the side for dipping.

7 | Enjoying More Laughter

The most wasted of all days is one without laughter.

E. E. CUMMINGS

FROM STEPHANIE

Becki, a great friend and coworker, tells this story: at an extended-family dinner one Christmas, we were all sitting at the table, from great-grandparents to the newest member of the family, my twenty-month-old nephew, Gavin, in his high chair. Great-grandpa said prayers, with all of us holding hands and bowing our heads. Being grateful for so many things, Grandpa prayed a little longer than usual. When we all said amen and raised our heads, peals of laughter rang out around the table. Little Gavin had the entire stick of butter from the butter dish and was devouring it!

■ ■ ■

"Mom, can I have some more water, please?" asked John as we were enjoying our dinner.

"Sure," I said, reaching for the water pitcher.

Jackson piped up, "Don't you mean 'goggin'?"

There was a momentary pause as our minds collectively whirred to make sense of what he was saying, and in unison our family dissolved in laughter. It wouldn't be funny to anyone else, but that's what made it all the more funny to us.

When our son John was just learning to talk, somehow he had adopted *goggin* as his own word for water. Whether it was water in a bathtub, rain from the sky, or a puddle on the ground, John, for the better part of a year, referred to it all as "goggin." We don't really know why, but our theory is that it had to do with the *gug, gug* sound of a watercooler.

Wherever the "word" came from, we hadn't thought about it, let alone uttered it, for years until Jackson seemingly pulled it out of our family's forgotten toddler lexicon.

What made it doubly funny was that Jackson hadn't even been born yet when John was asking for "goggin." He must have heard us talk about it at some point, and for reasons unexplained, he pulled it out on this particular evening.

As the laughter was waning and Les and I wiped the tears of laughter from our eyes, John reminded Jackson how he used to say "goyles" instead of girls. More laughter rolled out. Over the entire dinner we recounted stories of childhood quirks, including our own admissions, like the word *river*, which I pronounced "ribber" with total commitment and confidence until I was in the second grade.

As we said, there might not be another person on the earth who would find these words funny, but that's part of the joy that comes from inside humor around a family dinner table.

However you do it—with a joke, a well-timed tickle, or just a contagious case of the giggles—few things feel better than cracking up and laughing as a family. Laughing together warms relationships, smooths ruffled feathers, eases frustration, and releases tension. And, of course, any laughter, from the slightest chuckle to a sidesplitting howl, simply feels good.

Did You Know?

Families that share dinner together share more laughter! Research at Columbia University shows that kids who have regular family meals are half as likely to be highly stressed as those who rarely have dinner with their families.

HUMOR HELPS US COPE

Maybe you've heard the story about Janet. She wanted to impress a small group of friends with a fancy meal. She worked all day to cook a delectable meal, and she enlisted her husband's help to serve it. Everything went fine until it was time for the main course. As her husband was bringing in the crown roast, the kitchen door hit him from behind, and the platter flew across the room. Janet froze. Then after a moment, she regained her composure and said, "Dear, why don't you pick up that roast, go back into the kitchen, and get the *other* one!"

In case you didn't already know it—humor helps us

cope, not just with the trivial but even with the tragic. Psychoanalyst Martin Grotjahn, author of *Beyond Laughter*, notes that "to have a sense of humor is to have an understanding of human suffering."[1] And the life of Charlie Chaplin is a great illustration of this:

> *Chaplin grew up in the poorest section of London. His mother suffered from serious mental illness and his father died of alcoholism when Charlie was just five. Laughter was Chaplin's tool for coping with life's losses. Chaplin's eating a boiled leather shoe for dinner in his classic film* The Gold Rush *is more than a humorous scene. It is an act of human triumph, a monument to the coping power of humor.*[2]

If we are to be truthful, we have to admit that no family is immune to difficulties. We struggle with money issues, relationships, and schedules, to name just three. And for these struggles, and dozens of others, humor is invaluable.[3]

BRING A JOKE TO THE TABLE

"I've got a joke," said Jackson, our first grader, as we all sat down for dinner.

"Okay, let's hear it."

"What do aliens make in art class?" he asked with his quirky but contagious smile.

"I don't know," said John, our sixth grader. "What?"

"Spacecrafts."

A quick and easy way to bring more laughter to your dinner table is to have a joke in your hip pocket—by way of any number of family joke books. Of course, you'll want the age of your children to determine what you tell. Here are a few for any stage that will get you started (and if a family member is too young to "get it," that becomes all the more fun):

Q: What has more lives than a cat?
A: A frog—it croaks every night!

Q: What did one eye say to the other?
A: There is something between us that smells!

Q: What does a two-thousand-pound mouse say?
A: Here, kitty, kitty!

Q: What did the salad say to the refrigerator?
A: Close the door. I'm dressing!

Q: What do you get when you cross a bell and a chicken?
A: An alarm cluck.

By the way, you can also place a joke in your children's lunch boxes on occasion. They're sure to get a good laugh with their friends.

LAUGHING ALL THE WAY TO THE MILESTONE

Every life on this planet can be marked by milestones. The most celebrated, of course, are birthdays. Those are relatively easy. But

> Laughter is the most beautiful and beneficial therapy God ever granted humanity.
>
> CHUCK SWINDOLL

many other milestones are worthy of celebrations. We have educational milestones, such as starting or completing a particular grade or graduating from high school or college. We also have spiritual milestones, such as a child's first communion, dedication, or baptism. We have developmental milestones, such as sleeping in a "big boy" bed, learning to swim, getting a driver's license, or going on a first date. We have emotional milestones, such as moving past a bad habit (biting one's nails) or responding more maturely to siblings. Every child's life offers countless opportunities to celebrate.

Why should this matter? Because celebrations not only commemorate milestones worth remembering—they communicate a powerful message of love to a child, and they are a natural point for bringing more laughter into your home and to the dinner table.

Linda Click, of Adrian, Michigan, tells how for two months before her daughter Sandie's third birthday, the little girl said "I'm going to have a party" countless times a day. When the great event was finally over, Sandie told everyone, "I had a party." After several weeks, Linda and her husband grew weary of the repetition and finally told Sandie not to talk about the party anymore. For one whole day, Sandie didn't say a word about it. "But as I tucked her into bed that night," Linda explains, "Sandie prayed, 'Dear God, I had a birthday party.'"

Now there's one little girl who loves to be celebrated! But then, she isn't too different from any other child. Kids love celebrations because they cultivate fun and laughter and are tangible reminders that they are loved.

GOOD-HUMORED HIGH JINKS AT THE TABLE

FROM TINA

My kids think it is hilarious to play the "Mrs. Paghetti likes her spaghetti" game. It's a memory game, and each person has to repeat the previous sentences and add a new item at the end. For example, Mrs. Paghetti likes her spaghetti with meatballs. Next person: Mrs. Paghetti likes her spaghetti with meatballs and cheese. Next person: Mrs. Paghetti likes her spaghetti with meatballs, cheese, and cherries. The kids try to come up with random weird or even gross things, like ice cream, hot mustard, dirty socks—you get the picture. It may sound dumb, but they really do crack up when we do it—and it's a good memory game.

FROM STEPHANIE

When my kids were in grade school, I would always send green lunch-box food on St. Patrick's Day—green pistachio pudding, green celery sticks, green hard-boiled egg, green-colored mayo or peanut butter on their sandwiches, green sugar cookies, green milk, and a green napkin!

THROW A REVERSE SURPRISE PARTY

Surprise parties almost always bring lots of laughter into a home. But here's an idea you may never have considered: a surprise party in reverse.

Our friend Linda recently told us about a surprise party that happened on her eighth birthday. Her mother planned a breakfast surprise party—but Linda was in on the surprise. Her mom sent out invitations to Linda's friends' parents, cautioning, "Shh, it's a surprise birthday party for Linda, but we don't want your daughter to know." The parents kept the party a secret, and then at seven o'clock on Saturday morning, Linda's mom drove her minivan to each of the girls' homes. Linda, still in her pajamas, surprised them by waking them up. "Boy, were they surprised!" Linda says with a laugh, remembering the occasion as if it happened yesterday instead of some thirty years ago. "It was so fun to go and wake them up, and each friend I picked up got to participate in waking the next girl. Then we all went to my house in our pajamas!"

Instead of a cake, Linda's mom made birthday pancakes. She set out banana slices, strawberries, blueberries, chocolate chips, and whipped cream so the girls could decorate their pancakes. The morning ended with the girls painting picture frames for a group photo to commemorate the surprise.

It takes some creative thought to do something like this, but it's well worth the effort.

GETTING YOUR CARDIO AT THE DINNER TABLE

The late Norman Cousins, former editor of *Saturday Review*, subsequently professor at UCLA's School of Medicine, and author of *Anatomy of an Illness*, was the first to consider the scientific evidence of laughter's healing power. He called laughter "inner jogging." Why? Because every system in our bodies gets a workout when we enjoy a good laugh. Study after study has backed up Cousins's conclusions. Did you know, for example, that our cardiovascular and respiratory systems benefit more

Try This

Take turns going around the dinner table and asking one another to name things that move in the way of a named verb. For example:

- *What types of things mosey? Possible answers: older people, shoppers, cows in a field of dandelions, etc.*
- *What types of things speed? Possible answers: locomotives, race cars, jets, Superman, etc.*
- *Let each person give only one answer on each round until you've exhausted the possibilities.*

from twenty seconds of robust laughter than from three minutes of exercise on a rowing machine? Our muscles release tension when we laugh, and neurochemicals flow into our blood stream, creating the same feelings that long-distance joggers experience as "runner's high."[4]

And there is no better place to laugh than around the table together as a family. Just think: you can actually fit in a good workout while you're sitting at the table! So, lighten up. And enjoy the bond that grows from sharing laughter with those you love.

FROM STEPHANIE

My husband, Vern, cannot say "fajita." Whether we're at home or in a restaurant, he has to exaggerate

> Humor has a way of bringing people together. It unites people.
>
> RON DENTINGER

the pronunciation: "f-a-a-a *h-e-e-e-e* tah!" It always makes people laugh, and now, no one in the family can say it straight. Here is one of our favorite f-a-a-a *h-e-e-e-e* tah recipes. It also freezes well.

Chicken Fajitas (serves 6)

12 chicken breast tenders
1 large sliced yellow onion
1 sliced red bell pepper
1 sliced green bell pepper
¼ cup diced mild green chilies
¼ cup lime juice
1 teaspoon dried oregano
1 teaspoon kosher salt
½ teaspoon cumin
½ teaspoon pepper
12 six-inch flour or wheat tortillas
¼ cup oil

Add chicken, vegetables, and seasonings to an airtight container, and toss with lime juice to coat. Seal and marinate 24 to 48 hours in refrigerator or in freezer.

Before cooking, thaw if frozen. Wrap tortillas in foil and place in a warm oven. Heat the oil in a heavy, large sauté pan on stove top over medium-high heat. Add contents of chicken and vegetable container to pan, and stir-fry 10 to 12 minutes or until chicken is done. Serve with warm tortillas.

8 | Cultivating Deeper Values

What you do speaks so loudly that I cannot
hear what you say.

RALPH WALDO EMERSON

SALISH LODGE is a mountain retreat not far from our home in Seattle. It's one of our favorite places to eat. The dining room overlooks the breathtaking Snoqualmie Falls, and you can hear the roar of white water tumbling over granite cliffs nearly three hundred feet into the Emerald River canyon below.

Ranked one of the finest lodging and dining facilities in the world, the lodge has provided the backdrop for some very special moments in our lives. But one of our most meaningful Salish Lodge getaways came some years ago when we hired a babysitter to watch our three-year-old while we dedicated twenty-four hours of uninterrupted time to thinking about parenting. More specifically, we were thinking about the two of us as parents.

It started with a leisurely lunch the first day and ended

with a laid-back brunch on the second. In between, we enjoyed a scrumptious five-course dinner. At each of those meals, the topic of conversation was the same: what kinds of parents do we want to be—and what kind of kids do we want to raise?

We weren't talking about parenting techniques, philosophies, or strategies. We weren't discussing a parenting book or a class we had taken. We were exploring what we have come to call our "personal parenting traits." In other words, we were taking a hard look at our unique personalities and even the personalities of the parents who had raised us. Why? Because a wise mentor in our graduate-school days, while we were training to be psychologists, said something that stuck with us. "More important than what you *do* as a parent," he had said, "is who you *are* as a parent." He had gone on to explain that we can buy into any number of parenting strategies, but each and every one of them will be overshadowed by the personal qualities we bring to parenting.[1]

This is particularly true when it comes to passing along our values to our kids. Whether our children are trustworthy, dependable, kind, bold, careful, adventurous, committed, focused, open, playful, diligent, or whatever depends in great part on what qualities rub off from us. And here's why: because values are far more likely to be caught than taught. And that's what makes the family dinner table so crucial to this cause. No other ritual is more representative of where kids learn to embody their family's values than the one that takes place at the dinner table.

Of course every family holds different values and virtues. And even when we share a common value with others, we may prioritize it more or less than they do. That's why this chapter is not prescribing a set of values to you but simply exploring some of the most common ones and how they can be caught around the dinner table. After all, research shows that families who eat together are far more likely to hold the same values.

> Values demonstrate what we believe and hold dear. They can be religious, moral, social, or aesthetic. Values tell our children what is good, beneficial, important, useful, beautiful, and desirable.

WHAT DO YOU VALUE?

That's a big question, we know. After all, a list of potential values could fill every page of this book. But the more specific you can be in identifying the values you hold dear, the better you will be at passing them along to your children.

Here's a simple do-it-yourself exercise that will underscore the importance of identifying specific values.[2] Try it right now. It may not seem relevant at first, but trust us. Grab a pencil and a piece of paper. You'll also need a way to time yourself (a watch or clock with a second hand). If you want to see how this works, don't read any further until you have your pen or pencil, your paper, and your timer. Ready?

Step 1: Write down as many things that are white in color as you can think of. Start now, and stop in fifteen seconds.

Once you've done this, proceed to the next step.

Step 2: Write down as many white things in your refrigerator as you can think of. Start now, and stop in fifteen seconds.

How do your two lists compare?

Most people, remarkably, can list about as many white things from the small space of their refrigerator as they can when they consider the entire universe. Stunning, isn't it? Not only that, but when we confine our consideration of white things to the defined space of our refrigerator, the exercise is actually easier because concreteness helps our brains to focus more quickly and easily. The same holds true in listing our personal and family values. When it comes to the values we treasure, we recommend zeroing in on the categories where they are found. That way you'll be able to identify them more easily and specifically.

So, what is important to you in the following areas?

- Religious values
- Moral values
- Political values
- Social values
- Aesthetic values
- Health values
- Educational values

Other categories may come to mind as well. If so, great! Whatever your categories, identify a couple of values in each you hope your children will grow to embody.

TWO PREREQUISITES TO PASSING ON YOUR VALUES
The values you treasure most don't have a fighting chance of becoming a part of your children's character unless you

are doing two things: (1) building a bond of connection, and (2) giving an abundance of encouragement. Let's look at each of these ideas.

1. Connection

Values are predicated on connection. If you want to ensure that your children have the best chance of holding the values you treasure, you have to first and foremost connect with your children.

Look up the word *connect*, and you'll see it has several meanings. The one we're concerned with has to do with establishing rapport or relationship. Connected parents build a bond or link with their children, primarily through *communication*—a word that isn't far removed in its origin from the word *connection*. That's precisely why you hear people say, "Let's connect." What they really mean is, "Let's talk."

Our English word *communication* comes from the Latin word *communis*, which means "common." Makes sense, doesn't it? We are most connected when we find we have something in common with another person. The same is true in parent-child relationships. Parents who connect find ways to identify with their children because, when we have something in common, we join our hearts. We stand on common ground.

2. Encouragement

The late actress Celeste Holm said, "We live by encouragement and die without it—slowly, sadly, angrily." This is reason enough to bring an abundance of encouragement to every family meal, don't you think?

Encouragement is perhaps the finest gift we ever give our kids. When was the last time you served up a little encouragement? We recommend giving a healthy helping at every meal if you can. And although doing so doesn't cost a thing, what it does for your kids is priceless. Sidney Madwed says, "If everyone received the encouragement they need to grow, the genius in most everyone would blossom and the world would produce abundance beyond the wildest dreams. We would have more than one Einstein, Edison, Schweitzer, Mother Teresa, Dr. Salk, and other great minds in a century." [3]

Whether that is true or not, one thing is certain. Encouragement is sure to help your children become the kind of persons you hope they will be. It lowers their defenses. It makes meaningful connections more common. It sets the stage for them to absorb your values.

LOOKING FOR DIAMONDS

Do you want to know the secret to building a stronger family? A twenty-five-year study involving fourteen thousand families has attempted to reveal it. According to the study, successful families—those that avoid the daily dissension that often leads to fractured relationships— build a wall of appreciation and encouragement around themselves. Wow! Have you ever thought of it that way? Encouragement and appreciation are invaluable. "Strong families are good diamond hunters," says Nick Stinnett, lead researcher and professor of human development at the University of Alabama in Tuscaloosa. "They dig through the rough looking for the good in each other.

They build each other psychologically and realize that the need to be appreciated is one of the deepest needs we all have."[4]

Did You Know?

According to an article in Newsweek *magazine, "Eighty-one percent of mothers and 78 percent of fathers say they plan eventually to send their young child to Sunday school or some other kind of religious training."[5] Most parents sincerely want to raise children who are empathetic, know right from wrong, and attempt to follow the Golden Rule.*

HOW TO RAISE A LIAR

A recent issue of *New York* magazine ran a comprehensive article about research concerning kids and lying. In one study, researchers gathered a group of children together and read them a version of "The Boy Who Cried Wolf," the story in which a little boy is eaten by the wolf because he has lied so repeatedly that the villagers no longer trust him. In a survey of adults, taken before the study, most thought the negative consequences in "The Boy Who Cried Wolf" would lead the children to be more honest in controlled experiments on honesty and deceit.

However, after hearing the story, researchers observed that the children continued their usual rate of lying. Researchers then taught the story of George Washington and the cherry tree. In the story George goes to his father and confesses that he cut down the tree. His father replies,

"Hearing you tell the truth instead of a lie is better than if I had a thousand cherry trees." Researchers found that the story of George Washington and the cherry tree reduced lying by 43 percent.

> Kids learn our values when they feel free to ask questions.
>
> JANICE CROUSE

The conclusion? The researchers said that the threat of punishment simply teaches children to learn how to lie better. When children learn the worth of honesty, as they did in the story of George Washington, they lie less.[6]

Holding up your family values during a casual dinner conversation is superior to punishment. You can't goad or "guilt" a child into taking on character qualities you prize.

THE VALUE OF KNOWING GOD

Perhaps the most obvious family value is the most personal: a relationship with God. Of course, this can mean different things in different families, but for those families who practice religion, one thing is certain: God is present at the table. Not only that, but our children are probably more aware of this than we are.

Children, more than we know, have a connection to God that we don't always recognize. We love the story of a little girl named Sachi. Maybe you've heard it too.

Soon after her brother was born, little Sachi began to ask her parents to leave her alone with the new baby.

They worried that like most four-year-olds, she might
feel jealous and want to hit or shake him, so they said
no. But she showed no signs of jealousy. She treated the
baby with kindness and her pleas to be left alone with
him became more urgent. They decided to allow it.

Elated, she went into the baby's room and shut the
door, but it opened a crack—enough for her curious
parents to peek in and listen. They saw little Sachi
walk quietly up to her baby brother, put her face close
to his and say quietly, "Baby, tell me what God feels
like. I'm starting to forget." [7]

Apocryphal or not, this story reminds us that as we grow
older, we lose some of our heartstrings—the ones that tie us
to God. Life can't help but become more cluttered, and if we
aren't intentional, we soon forget what God "feels" like.

Did You Know?

According to a survey from the Barna Research Group,
about two out of three parents of children under age
twelve attend religious services at least once a month and
generally take their children with them. [8] *However, the*
survey of 1,010 adults found that most parents have no
plan for cultivating the spiritual values and the spiritual
development of their children.

THE VALUE OF GENEROSITY

All it took was a simple challenge over dinner one night:
we gave our boys one dollar each and asked, "What can

you do with this to make a difference?" This invitation seemed to ignite their generous spirits.

In the midst of Seattle's cold winter rains, our twelve-year-old son, John, and his eight-year-old brother, Jackson, put their heads together and rounded up a small circle of friends. That evening, before the challenge, John had heard a local news report about the nomadic residents of Seattle's "Tent City," an enclave of tightly orga-nized homeless travelers who found temporary respite on the host grounds of churches and community centers, camping for a few weeks at a time and then moving on.

The boys and their buddies decided the residents of Tent City would enjoy a warm meal served indoors. With the help of some parents, the boys each baked their favor-ite cookies, prepared warm cocoa, and added their per-sonal savings to buy batteries (important to people with no electricity) and socks and hand warmers and blankets and personal items.

Our families gathered to serve a chicken dinner and share conversations around the tables while the boys took plates of cookies around to each guest, with huge grins and warmed hearts. As parents, we felt our own hearts warmed even more when we saw those boys doing huge stacks of dishes in the commercial-size kitchen of the host church.

Later that week when John shared his experience at Tent City in his Boy Scout troop meeting, his joy was so contagious that his fellow Scouts asked if they could find a way to do the same thing as a group.

A generous spirit is contagious—even for kids.

THE VALUE OF WISE CHOICES

The Cosby Show was one of television's biggest hits in the 1980s. Based on the comedy of Bill Cosby, *The Cosby Show* told the story of the Huxtables, an upper-middle-class African American family in Brooklyn, New York. In a scene from the pilot episode, the son, Theo, brings home a report card with four Ds. When his father, Cliff, is upset, Theo explains that he doesn't plan on going to college. He simply wants to be a "regular person"—to make money and live life however he wants to live it. Recognizing a teaching moment is at hand, Cliff offers his son a lesson in the cost of living for "regular people."

"So, how much do you expect to make a week as a 'regular person'?" Cliff asks.

"$250," Theo replies.

Cliff points to the bed. "Sit down, son."

Theo and Cliff both sit on Theo's bed. Cliff pulls out a stack of Monopoly money. "I will give you $300 a week. That's $1,200 a month."

Cliff hands Theo the money. Theo rifles through it with a grin on his face. "I'll take it!" he says.

"And I will take $350 for taxes," Cliff fires back, taking a few bills from Theo's hands.

"Whoa!" Theo says.

"Oh, yeah. You see—the government goes for the 'regular people' first. So, how much does that leave you with?"

Theo counts his money. "$850."

"Okay, now you'll need an apartment because you are *not* living here. An apartment in Manhattan will run you at least $400 a month." Cliff reaches over and takes another $400 from Theo.

"I'll live in New Jersey," Theo says, as he takes back $200.

"Now you'll need a car!" Cliff takes $300.

"I'll drive a motorbike," Theo says, taking back $100.

"Well, you're going to need a helmet," Cliff says, taking $50 from Theo's hand. "Now, figure $100 a month for clothes and shoes."

"Figure $200?" Theo says. "I want to look *good!*"

"So, how much does that leave you with?" Cliff asks.

"$200. So, no problem!"

"There *is* a problem—you haven't eaten yet!" With that, Cliff takes another $100.

"I can get by on bologna and cereal," Theo says, taking back $100. "So I've got everything under control *plus* $200 left for the month."

"You plan to have a girlfriend?" Cliff asks.

"For sure!"

Cliff takes the remaining $200. He points to Theo's empty hand and says, "Regular people."[9]

Did You Know?

Among teens who had dinner with their families five or more nights a week, 86 percent reported they had never tried smoking, compared with 65 percent of youth who had dinner with their families two or fewer nights a week. Similarly, teens who ate dinner with their families five or more nights a week were less likely to have tried alcohol or marijuana. Teens who had frequent family dinners were also more likely to get better grades.[10]

THE VALUE OF PATIENCE

Sometime ago, over boiled eggs and bagels, I (Leslie) was helping our older son review his spelling words—the ones we had worked on the night before. When he made the same mistake three times in a row, I found myself saying sternly, "John, think! Sound out the word! *A-s-t-r-o-n-a-u-t*. We did this just last night, and you knew it then."

Tears welled up in John's eyes, and he looked panicked and desperate. Though I hadn't intended to spoil his breakfast or his confidence, that's what I did. That's what impatience can do to a child. It doesn't matter that I felt tired and pressured by the clock. What John knew is that I lost my patience.

Do you know what tops the list of skills parents need most? According to a recent study by York University, it's . . . wait for it . . . wait for it . . . patience. What's more, impatience was the number one attitude they did not want to pass on to their children.[11]

No big surprise, right? After all, patience, according to many experts, is one of the most important traits a parent can master in raising kids. How important is patience to parenting? Let's put it this way: it's impossible to be a loving parent without an abundance of patience. It's so important that the apostle Paul began his famous love poem, in 1 Corinthians 13, with "Love is patient."

THE VALUE OF KEEPING YOUR WORD

One evening John and Jackson had been in bed for at least an hour when Leslie and I returned from a dinner out with friends. We debriefed with the babysitter and then sneaked into the boys' room to kiss them good night.

"Dad, can I have some ice cream?" Jackson whispered.

"No, Jack, it's late, way past bedtime."

"But, Daddy, you promised you'd get ice cream while you were gone."

He was right. Jack had asked for ice cream earlier in the day, but we didn't have any. So I had told him, "If you eat up all your green beans, I'll get some for you while I'm out—I promise."

Dinnertime for the boys came and went. We cleaned up the kitchen; the boys picked up their toys. The sitter arrived. And Leslie and I left for our evening with friends.

> # Strength of character may be acquired at work, but beauty of character is learned at home.
>
> HENRY DRUMMOND

I'd forgotten all about the ice cream. But Jackson hadn't.

So even though it was after ten o'clock, I hopped in the car, drove to the grocery store, bought a pint of cookies-and-cream, and hurried home. Jack and I enjoyed a late-night bowl together. Why? Because I had promised. And I want my sons to grow up seeing their dad keep his word. I want them to know that they can count on me—that I'm sincere, genuine, and trustworthy.[12]

LOOK WHO'S COMING TO DINNER

A surprisingly powerful way to cultivate your values in your child is by having dinner guests who embody or represent those values.

Here are a few examples:

- ◆ Grandparents can underscore the value of family.
- ◆ Clergy can underscore the value of relating to God.
- ◆ Teachers can underscore the value of education.
- ◆ Neighbors can underscore the value of relationships.
- ◆ International persons can underscore the value of a global perspective.

Some time ago we were guests in the home of Rabbi Daniel Lapin. Rabbi Lapin and his wife, Susan, had invited us to join them, two of their six daughters, and some of their Jewish friends for Shabbat (the Jewish Sabbath). We had never been to a Shabbat before, so we were eager to learn, and the Lapin family members were great teachers. Jewish tradition encourages hospitable community, and the Lapins, while deeply rooted in their Orthodox Jewish community, are an open door of hospitality.

The Lapins live on Mercer Island, a part of Seattle, in a neighborhood defined by faith. Because all labor is forbidden on Shabbat, everyone who attends synagogue must live within easy walking distance. We drove to Mercer Island from our home in downtown Seattle and felt strangely conspicuous slamming our car doors as the other guests arrived on foot. We gathered around the candlelit table and engaged in a wonderful ceremony of worship as we ate. One of the first things we did was to wash our hands together in a period of silence. That was followed by the breaking and blessing of the bread. Hebrew is the predominant language of worship, but our hosts graciously included English commentary. There is wine and a blessing.

During the meal, only one central conversation is cultivated; no side comments or one-on-one talking with those seated near you is allowed. I learned the lesson quietly when I (Leslie) was gently scolded for drifting off into an impromptu conversation with my neighbor. Rabbi Lapin sprinkled the meal with wise homily based on Torah readings and Jewish tradition. The meal is simultaneously scripted and spontaneous. The order and timing of the meal are disciplined, but that produces a strange freedom. Listening so intently in a group, engaging together as the rabbi directed questions to each of us with the entire table listening in, created a delightful and higher level of conversation our family won't soon forget.[13]

THE VALUE OF LOVE

The animated movie *Cloudy with a Chance of Meatballs* tells the story of Flint Lockwood, a young inventor who dreams of creating something that will improve everyone's life in the town of Swallow Falls, which is known only for its sardines. When Flint creates a machine that can turn water into food, he decides to test it out. The test goes poorly—he accidentally destroys the town square—and Flint assumes his inventing career is over. But then something amazing happens: cheeseburgers start raining from the sky. His machine works!

The movie shows many more adventures—and misfortunes—that come about because of this invention, but it's another invention created by Flint that is the envy of any parent who struggles to express love. Over the course of the movie, we learn that ever since his mother's death, Flint has longed for his father's love and affirmation. But like many fathers who have trouble expressing themselves to their kids, Flint's father, Tim, struggles to connect with his son. When Tim does try to communicate with Flint, he opts for fishing metaphors that leave Flint confused and even hurt.

Strangely enough, Flint's monkey assistant, Steve, is there to help. In order to communicate, Steve wears a "monkey thought translator" that Flint created. When Steve wants to tell Flint something, he simply thinks it, and the translator speaks it. Near the end of the movie, after Flint has saved the city from destruction brought about because of his machine, Tim tries to tell Flint how he feels—how proud he is—but once again, he just can't quite communicate his love.

"Flint, uhh . . . When you, uhh . . . When you cast your line, if it's not straight, uhh . . . "

After stumbling to find the words—the right metaphor— Flint's father, Tim, gives up.

Suddenly Sam, Flint's girlfriend, snatches the monkey thought translator from around Steve's neck and places it on Tim. Immediately Tim can express his real thoughts. "I'm proud of you, Flint," Tim says. "I'm amazed that someone as ordinary as me could be the father of someone as extraordinary as you. You're talented. You're a total original. Your lab is breathtaking. Your mom—she always knew you were going to be special. If she were here today, she'd tell us both, 'I told you so.' So now, when I take this thing off, and you hear me make a fishing metaphor, just know that fishing metaphor means 'I love you.'"

"I love you too, Dad," Flint replies.

Of course, in real life, there are no magical translators for parents. But the challenge is ours just the same: to find ways to clearly and even creatively speak and embody love to the sons and daughters we have been gifted with.[14]

RULES AND RELATIONSHIPS

In a study of teenagers regarding degrees of honesty and deceit, researchers found that most parents believe being permissive will encourage openness and honesty from their kids. Parents of teenagers would rather be informed than strict and "in the dark." However, researchers discovered that a "no rules" policy simply doesn't work.[15]

One researcher noted, "Kids who go wild and get in trouble mostly have parents who don't set rules or standards. Their parents are loving and accepting no matter what the kids do. But the kids take the lack of rules as a sign their parents don't care—that their parent doesn't really want the job of being the parent. . . . Ironically, the type of parents who are actually most consistent in enforcing rules are the same parents who are most warm and have the most conversations with their kids."[16]

Though some rules result in arguments between parents and teens, only 23 percent of the teenagers surveyed considered these conflicts harmful to their relationship with their parents.

MAXIMIZING THE ODDS OF CULTIVATING DEEP VALUES

Some time ago, we attended a conference in Atlanta and heard Tim Sanders, former chief solutions officer at Yahoo! and author of *Today We Are Rich*, speak. In his remarks he shared a piece on priorities that got us thinking.

"Take your life and all the things that you think are important, and put them in one of three categories," Tim suggested. Then he gave us the categories. They were represented by three items: glass, metal, and rubber.

When you drop the things that are made of rubber, Tim said, they will bounce back. Nothing really happens when these kinds of things get dropped. So, for instance, if you miss your favorite team's game, your life will bounce back just fine. Nothing of consequence changes, and nothing is lost. Missing a game, or even a whole season of football, will not alter your family relationships or your spiritual life.

When things made of metal are dropped, they create a lot of noise. But you can recover from the drop. If you miss a meeting at work, you can get the notes from a colleague. If you forget to balance your checkbook and the bank notifies you that you have been spending more than you have, that's going to create a little bit of noise in your life, but you can recover from it.

Then there are things made of glass. And when you drop one of these, it will shatter into pieces and never be the same. Even though you try to put it back together, it will still be missing some pieces. It certainly won't look the same, and it probably won't function the same way because the consequences of its being broken will forever affect how it's used.

Once Tim shared these vivid images with the audience, the room was hushed. He leaned over the podium and said this: "You're the only person who knows what those things are that you can't afford to drop. More than likely, they have a lot to do with your relationships. Your family."

We doubt you'd argue with that. The very fact that you're reading this book tells us that your family is a priority. So, are you cultivating the character qualities that matter most in your children? Are you giving them the routine of a family dinner hour to maximize the chances that they will catch the values you hold dear?

FROM STEPHANIE

When my kids were young, the least expensive and most memorable vacation was to go camping. The unplugged experience without the commitments of home and regular chores are some of my children's favorite memories. None of us will forget the night where the light from a full moon was like a giant flashlight beam. We all played on the beach for hours making moon shadows, then went swimming at midnight.

Camping dinners were always delicious no matter what you served. After a full day of playing in the fresh air, almost anything cooked on the grill was delicious. What follows is one of our favorites. If you make it up and freeze it ahead of time, it not only is a meal but helps to keep the ice chest cold.

Smoky Sausage and Cheddar Potatoes
(serves 6)

5 cups diced potatoes
½ teaspoon kosher salt
2 tablespoons olive oil
2 tablespoons cooked bacon bits
2 tablespoons chopped green onions
1 pound cubed smoked kielbasa
1 cup shredded smoked cheddar cheese

Place potatoes in the middle of an 18-inch length of heavy aluminum foil. Cover with remaining ingredients in the order given. Wrap foil tightly to seal. (If you are going to freeze this, thaw completely before the next step.) Bake over medium heat on a grill or in a 375° oven for 45 to 60 minutes or until potatoes are tender.

9 | Instilling Gentle Manners

Nothing is less important than which fork you use.
Etiquette is the science of living. It embraces everything.
It is ethics. It is honor.
EMILY POST

Mom never put a bottle of ketchup on the table. She'd spoon the ketchup into a little dish, and we'd spoon it onto our burgers or hot dogs. It didn't matter how informal the meal was—just Mom, my two brothers, Dad, and me around the kitchen table.

"C'mon, Mom," I remember saying on occasion. "Why don't you just put the bottle on the table?"

"It's nicer this way, honey," she'd say.

And I suppose it was. I, like my brothers, came to accept the way Mom did things like this at the dinner table. She was never pushy about it. I don't remember ever being corrected for having my elbows on the table or for not sitting up straight in my chair or being scolded for chewing with my mouth open. But looking back on my childhood and our family dinnertimes, I quietly and gently absorbed the proper way to behave.

In fact, I absorbed it so well that I remember coming into our tiny apartment kitchen shortly after Leslie and I were married and discovering that Leslie had set the table for dinner and placed a big squeezable bottle of Heinz ketchup in the middle of it. *How can this be*? I wondered. *That's not the way to serve ketchup!*

That's the way of gentle manners and etiquette. They simply rub off. No need for snippy lessons or harsh scolding. Children can learn their manners without making a meal an emotional mess. In this chapter we'll show you how.

JUST A LITTLE R-E-S-P-E-C-T

George Bernard Shaw gave an ancient Greek legend a twentieth-century twist when he retold the story of *Pygmalion*.[1] Shaw's adaptation features a professor, Henry Higgins, who is the world's leading authority on speech and diction. Higgins often coaches London's elite in speech and deportment, and the professor's friend, Colonel Pickering, bets Higgins that he cannot take a Cockney flower girl and pass her off as a lady after just three months of instruction. This challenge is too much to resist for the haughty professor, and he chooses Eliza Doolittle as the object of his experiment.

With drills, lessons, and insensitive threats, Higgins drives Eliza like a slave master. At one point Higgins says, "Eliza, you're an idiot." Pickering tries to buffer the professor's treatment of Eliza, but to Higgins, Eliza is nothing but a laboratory experiment.

The great day arrives, and Higgins unveils his "experiment" at a royal reception. Eliza enters wearing jewels and a lovely gown. She walks gracefully, demonstrates impeccable manners. Her diction is pure, and her conversation is refined. In short order, Eliza becomes the toast of London.

After the reception, as Higgins and Pickering unwind in the study, they hardly notice Eliza. Finally she confronts the mighty professor: yes, he may have changed her dialect, but the kindness of Colonel Pickering changed her heart. He is the real Pygmalion. His gentle affirmation is what truly made the difference.

Eliza then says to Colonel Pickering, "I owe so much to you. . . . It was from you that I learned really nice manners, and that's what makes one a lady, isn't it?"

Pickering bashfully responds, "No doubt. Still he taught you to speak, you know, and I couldn't have done that."

"Of course," Eliza continues. "But you know what began my real education? Your calling me 'Miss Doolittle' that day when I first came to the professor's study. That was the beginning of self-respect for me. You see, the difference between a lady and a flower girl isn't how she behaves. It's how she is treated. I know that I shall always be a flower girl to Professor Higgins because he always treats me as a flower girl and always will. But I know that I can be a lady to you because you always treat me as a lady and always will."[2]

There you have it. The gentle way wins. It's key to instilling etiquette and good manners in your children. You may get them to "behave" around you when you scold them into it, but you'll get them to become little gentlemen or ladies when you treat them with respect. It has more to do with how they are treated than how they behave.

HOW TO RESPECT YOUR CHILD

The word *respect* has its origins in the words *respite* and *refuge*. When we show our children respect, we make them feel safe—and that safety allows them to become better persons.

The fact that children are sometimes irrational (by virtue of the fact that their brains are still developing) and inexperienced doesn't mean they don't deserve your respect. They may not have earned it, but they still *deserve* it.

So how do you show respect to your children? You certainly show respect when you make eye contact and listen, when you knock before entering their rooms, when you say please and thank you, when you ask their opinions, and so on. In short, showing respect comes down to the Golden Rule: treat your children as you would like to be treated . . . and they will likely eventually treat you with respect too. Sure, this will sometimes call on every ounce of maturity you can muster, but you can do this. "If you have some respect for people as they are," says John W. Gardner, "you can be more effective in helping them to become better than they are."

Did You Know?

Some think the expression "Mind your p's and q's" originated in British pubs as an abbreviation for "Mind your pints and quarts." Supposedly this warned the barkeep to serve full measure, mark the customer's tab accurately, and so on. But the expression actually refers to the difficulty children have distinguishing lowercase p and q, which are mirror images of each other. Mind your you-know-whats was thus a teacher's admonition to students and became a colloquialism for being well mannered.

MANNERS COME FROM MANAGING EMOTIONS

Not far from our home in Seattle is a world-renowned center for research on parent-child interactions. The center is directed by Dr. John Gottman at the University of Washington. He and his team have conducted in-depth research into 119 families, observing how parents and children relate to one another. He has followed these children from age four to adolescence. His studies involve lengthy interviews with parents about their marriages, their reactions to their children's emotional experiences, and their own awareness of their roles in their children's lives. He has checked in with these families over time to see how the children are developing in terms of health, academic achievement, emotional development, and social relationships.

His results tell a simple yet compelling story. He has found that most parents fall into one of two broad categories: those who give their children guidance about the world of emotion and those who don't. He calls the parents who get involved with their children's feelings "Emotion Coaches." You might say that these parents go out of their way to respect their children's feelings.

Much like athletic coaches, they study their children and teach them how to deal with life. They don't object to their children's displays of anger, sadness, or fear. Nor do they ignore them. Instead, they accept negative emotions as a fact of life and use emotional moments as opportunities to teach their kids important life lessons.

Did You Know?

Your bread plate always goes on your left, and your drink always goes on your right. A good way to remember this rule is to remember that the word drink *starts with the letters* D *and* R *for "drinks right."*

What difference does it make when children have parents who respect their feelings? By observing and analyzing in detail the words, actions, and emotional responses of families over time, Dr. Gottman has discovered a truly significant contrast. Children whose parents consistently practice Emotion Coaching have better physical health and score higher academically than children whose parents don't offer such guidance. These kids get along better with friends, have fewer behavioral problems, and are less prone to acts of violence. Overall, these children are well behaved, have good manners, and experience fewer negative feelings and more positive feelings. In short, they're healthier mentally, physically, and spiritually.[3]

But the result that has surprised Dr. Gottman most is this: when mothers and fathers work to intentionally respect their children's emotions, the children are "better able to soothe themselves, bounce back from distress, and carry on with productive activities."[4] In other words, they are not just well mannered, they are becoming emotionally intelligent.

KIDS GONE WILD?

In a recent survey by Public Agenda, a nonprofit research group, only 9 percent of adults were able to say the children they saw in public were respectful toward adults. More than one out of three teachers considered leaving their profession or were acquainted with another teacher who quit. The reason? Students' "intolerable behavior." And in an Associated Press poll, 70 percent of respondents declared that "people are ruder than they were 20 or 30 years ago." Among the worst offenders: children.[5]

Why? You may not like the answer. Experts say it's because of what parents expect from kids. These experts say that "the pressure to do well is up. The demand to do *good* is down." Way down.

> Manners are a sensitive awareness of the feelings of others. If you have that awareness, you have good manners, no matter which fork you use.
>
> EMILY POST

Harvard University child psychologist Dan Kindlon believes "Most parents would like their children to be polite, considerate, and well behaved. But they're too tired, worn down by work and personally needy to take up the task of teaching them proper behavior at home."[6] He also observes that present-day parenting has much to do with training boys and girls to compete in school or on the soccer field. But competition doesn't teach civility.

GOOD MANNERS 101

It's been said that the test of good manners is to be patient with bad ones. We agree. But that doesn't mean you don't let your kids know what good manners are. Of course, the topic has filled dozens of books, but the following are a few of the basics to keep "on the table":

- Don't chew with your mouth open.
- Don't reach for an item that is not right in front of you. Ask someone to pass it. And if you are passing something, don't help yourself along the way. Wait for the other person to pass it back.
- If your food is too hot, wait for it to cool. Don't blow on it.
- Don't talk with your mouth full.
- Bring your food up to your mouth rather than bend over the plate or bowl to reach it.
- Don't run your fingers through your hair at the table.
- Don't come to the table without a shirt.
- Take your cap off at the table.
- Don't slurp anything.

- Pass salt and pepper shakers together (they never separate).
- During the meal if you need to visit the restroom, simply say, "Excuse me for a moment; I'll be right back."
- Begin to eat only after everyone has been seated at the table.
- Before leaving the table, thank the person who prepared the meal.
- Keep your elbows off the table while eating.

Did You Know?

A handshake originally was meant to show that men were not carrying a sword or knife in their hands. You can use this tidbit to teach your little boy or girl to offer a good handshake and some eye contact while saying, "It's nice to meet you."

GOOD MANNERS REQUIRE KINDNESS

We were serving a family favorite for dessert one evening—mint-chip ice-cream pie with a chocolate graham-cracker crust. As it was being set in the middle of the table, Jackson piped up, "I want the biggest piece!"

"Jack," John responded, "it's not polite to ask for the biggest piece."

Jackson paused for a moment and asked, "Well, then, how do you get it?"[7]

That's a good question. And one that holds a lesson in unselfishness. After all, good manners are all about kindness and civility—not looking out for number one. Of course, this is something that doesn't come naturally to a seven-year-old, or even to a forty-seven-year-old. We are all works in progress when it comes to putting other people's needs ahead of our own. That's why this is a trait that will be caught as well as taught. The more parents model a bit of self-sacrifice, the more your children will embody it.

When Chuck Swindoll was asked how he worked to become less selfish, he said, "Very simple: God gives me four busy kids who step on shoes, wrinkle clothes, spill milk, lick car windows, and drop sticky candy on the carpet. . . . Being unselfish in attitude strikes at the very core of our being. It means we are willing to forgo our own comfort, our own preferences, our own schedule, our own desires."[8]

That's so true. And that self-sacrifice we make as parents, when made with loving hearts, teaches our children far more character qualities than just politeness. It engenders a deep kindness and a gracious spirit in our children, who then can't help but be well mannered.

Try This

When you ask for a dish at the table to be passed to you, offer it to others before serving yourself. You can say, "Would anyone else like more potatoes before I help myself?" You may not get any takers, but that's not the point. This kind question, and the generosity it represents, will rub off on your children, and over time they'll be doing the same thing.

ADVANCED ETIQUETTE

If you want to take the practice of etiquette to a higher level around your dinner table and join the ranks of the truly refined, here are some additional proper pointers:

- ◆ After you pick up a piece of cutlery, it should never touch the table again. Knives go on the plate, blade facing in and touching the inside of the plate. Only the handle should rest on the rim of the plate.
- ◆ Don't flap your napkin to unfold it, and don't wave it around like a flag. It belongs partially unfolded on your lap. If you leave the table, place your napkin on the chair (not on the table) and push the chair back under the table.
- ◆ Tear bread into bite-size pieces and butter each piece just before you eat it. Don't butter the entire slice of bread or the entire roll to get it ready for occasional bites during the course of the meal. The same holds true for jam.[9]

Of course, holding your pinkie—as well as your nose—in the air while you sip a spot of tea is purely optional.

WHAT NOT TO TALK ABOUT AT THE TABLE

Augustine, one of the early Christian church fathers, encouraged conversation at meals—but with a strictly enforced rule. It's a rule that, all these years later, might not be bad for most modern families to follow. Augustine wanted to be sure that the character of an absent person would never be negatively discussed. And he wasn't joking.

He actually had the rule to this effect carved on a plaque attached to his table.

Not a bad idea, don't you think? Not the plaque, but the rule.

Good conversation skills are among the most important manners your children can learn. So why not follow Augustine's lead and decide in advance what you won't talk about at the table. We have friends who have agreed never to talk about work issues at the dinner table. The famed Kennedy family had a rule never to talk about money at dinner.

So consider those topics in your family that are likely to lead to an unproductive conversation. Maybe it's bringing up homework assignments. Maybe it has to do with household chores. Or maybe it's a character trait that drives one of you nuts. Whatever the topics, recognize that they would impair the kind of conversation you'd like to have as you enjoy your mealtimes together, and steer clear of those topics.[10]

ESTABLISH SOME HOUSE RULES

Every home has its own way of doing things when it comes to table manners. What's important to you may not be to others. What is important is that your kids know what you expect. Here are a few house rules you may want to consider and add to:

- Wash your hands before you come to the table.
- Take your dirty dishes to the kitchen sink.
- No reading, talking on cell phones, or texting at the table.

- No toys or pets at the table.
- Wait your turn to talk (don't interrupt others).
- Ask to be excused before leaving the table after the meal.

GIVE UP THE GULP-AND-GO

Leaning over your plate, scooping food into your mouth, and neglecting the people you're eating with is just plain rude. But it happens in families every day. We've become so accustomed to fast food that we've forgotten the civility of savoring our time at the table.

> Children are natural mimics who act like their parents despite every effort to teach them good manners.
>
> ANONYMOUS

Believe it or not, there is actually an official "Slow Food" movement. It began in 1986 when McDonald's opened a restaurant beside the famous Spanish Steps in Rome, Italy. For the locals, this fast-food step crossed the line, and Carlo Petrini, a culinary writer, began a campaign. He wanted to defend good taste, and he said it would "begin at the table of Slow Food."[11]

So how do you savor your food? You simply slow down and pay attention to it. The same holds true of your family, by the way. You will savor your relationships when you slow down and pay attention to them, act civilly, demonstrate kindness, and display good manners. The point is that this is precious time. You can't take it for granted. It is precious.

HOW TO SET A TABLE

One of the great traditions of a family dinner for many parents is getting the kids involved in setting the table. This preamble to the meal not only serves a valuable function but starts to gather the family together for the meal to come. And if your kids are going to take on this responsibility, you might as well teach them to do it right, right? The diagram below can help you to do that.

Silverware is put in the order it will be needed. Items used first (such as salad forks and soupspoons) go on the outside. There are a few exceptions. For example, dessert silverware goes above the plate. Kids can adjust what they set based on the meal. No soup? Don't put out the soupspoons.

By the way, tablecloths and place mats can provide an easy cleanup, but there is no rule of etiquette for table covers at casual meals, so the choice is completely yours. The point is that having a table set correctly before the meal helps to make the meal more peaceful and pleasant because it eliminates the need for family members to leave the table to get things after the meal has started.

Try This

*One thing you may consider while teaching your child
how to set the table is making place mats from heavy
paper (such as shopping bags) and drawing pictures of
forks, knives, spoons, and so on in the places where they
should be set. This is an especially fun way to teach your
young child about setting the table. They can draw in the
utensils, napkin, plate, and glass on the place mat and
then customize each place mat for each family member
with crayons, markers, or colored pencils.*

FROM STEPHANIE

One evening my daughter came home in disgust after
having dinner at a friend's home. "They ate their pork
chops with their hands!" she exclaimed. We had to have
a discussion about how every family is different and has
different rules, not right or wrong, just different. Whatever
your family rule, we hope you enjoy the zesty pork chops
on the next page.

Zesty Lemon Pork Chops (serves 6)

6 boneless pork chops
²/₃ cup lemonade concentrate
²/₃ cup barbecue sauce
2 dashes of Tabasco sauce
1 teaspoon pepper

Blend lemonade concentrate, sauces, and pepper in an airtight container. Add pork chops, and toss to coat. Seal and refrigerate for 24 hours, or freeze.

Before cooking, thaw completely if frozen. Remove pork chops from marinade, and grill or pan fry for 3 to 5 minutes per side, brushing with marinade before turning.

10 | Counting Your Blessings

We can only be said to be alive in those moments when
our hearts are conscious of our treasures.

THORNTON WILDER

WHEN I (LES) was a kid growing up in Boston, my family
would sometimes visit the quaint town of Stockbridge,
Massachusetts. It was the home of Norman Rockwell—
and I've always loved his paintings. In fact, on one visit
we actually had the honor of meeting the famed painter,
and he showed us a bit of his studio. That's where I saw
the original of a print we had in our home. You've probably seen it. It depicts a nicely dressed elderly woman and,
presumably, her grandson huddled together at the corner
of a table, about to have lunch in a crowded restaurant.
They both have their heads bowed, and their hands are
clasped in front of them. On the other side of the table
from them are two young bucks, one of whom has a
cigarette dangling from his mouth. They're observing

the woman and boy as if they've never seen two people pray before. The title of the painting is *Saying Grace*. And it's a powerful reminder of the dignity and beauty of this hallowed tradition.[1]

Maybe you already pray a word of thanks before your meals. Millions of people do. The dinner hour is a terrific time to take a moment as a family and count your blessings. In fact, this single act around the table—whatever your faith perspective—just may be the most important part of your meal. Research reveals that systematically focusing on wanting what we have—not having what we want—does more to lift the quality of our lives than any other measurable emotion.

THERE'S NO RIGHT OR WRONG WAY TO SAY GRACE

Some time ago we heard a story that's been circulating of a six-year-old boy who asked if he could say grace at a restaurant. His family bowed their heads, and he prayed, "God is good. God is great. Thank you for the food, and I would even thank you more if Mom gets us ice cream for dessert. And liberty and justice for all! Amen!"

Whether that really happened or not, we have to say

A SIMPLE PRAYER OF THANKS

If you're looking for a little guidance in initiating the tradition of saying grace, here's a common prayer that will help you humbly offer your gratitude:

> For food in a world where many walk in hunger,
> For friends in a world where many walk alone,
> For faith in a world where many walk in fear,
> We give you thanks, O Lord. Amen.

that the best prayers are generally unscripted and come straight from the heart. Whether it's coming from a parent or the youngest child at the table, you can never go wrong with a heartfelt word of grace where you pray for one another, and give thanks for the food. It's a loving and warm way to start a meal and a great way to join your spirits. Oh, and if it fits your style, don't forget to incorporate a little touch by holding hands while you say grace.

WHOSE SHOULDERS ARE YOU SITTING ON?

Jewish poet and storyteller Noah ben Shea tells a parable that serves as a powerful reminder of an important truth.

> *After a meal, some children turned to their father, Jacob, and asked if he would tell them a story. "A story about what?" asked Jacob.*
>
> *"About a giant," squealed the children.*
>
> *Jacob smiled, leaned against the warm stones at the side of the fireplace, and his voice turned softly inward. "Once there was a boy who asked his father to take him to see the great parade that passed through the village. The father, remembering the parade from when he was a boy, quickly agreed, and the next morning the boy and his father set out together. As they approached the parade route, people started to push in from all sides, and the crowd grew thick. When the people along the way became almost a wall, the father lifted his son and placed him on his shoulders."*

THE HOUR THAT MATTERS MOST

"What happened next?" a little boy asked Jacob.

"Soon the parade began, and as it passed, the boy kept telling his father how wonderful it was and how spectacular were the colors and images. The boy, in fact, grew so prideful of what he saw that he mocked those who saw less, saying, even to his father, 'If only you could see what I see.'"

"But," said Jacob, staring straight in the faces of the children, "what the boy did not look at was why he could see. What the boy forgot was that once his father, too, could see."

Then, as if he had finished the story, Jacob stopped speaking.

"Is that it?" said a disappointed girl. "We thought you were going to tell us a story about a giant."

"But I did," said Jacob. "I told you a story about a boy who could have been a giant."

"How?" squealed the children.

"A giant," said Jacob, "is anyone who remembers we are all sitting on someone else's shoulders."

"And what does it make us if we don't remember?" asked the boy.

"A burden," answered Jacob. [2]

This is the secret of gratitude: humility. As William Gurnall says, "Humility is a necessary veil to all other graces."

> Gratitude helps you to grow and expand; gratitude brings joy and laughter into your life and into the lives of all those around you.
> **EILEEN CADDY**

When we remember that we are sitting on someone else's shoulders we can't help but be grateful.

THE KEY TO HAPPINESS

Dr. Robert Emmons, professor of psychology at the University of California, Davis, and Dr. Michael McCullough, psychology professor at the University of Miami, have long been interested in the role gratitude plays in physical and emotional well-being. They took three groups of volunteers and randomly assigned them to focus on one of three things each week: hassles, things for which they were grateful, and ordinary life events.

The first group concentrated on everything that went wrong or irritated them. The second group focused on situations they felt enhanced their lives, such as, "My mom is so kind and caring—I'm lucky to have her." The third group recalled recent everyday events, such as, "I went shoe shopping."

The results: the people who focused on gratitude were happier. They saw their lives in favorable terms. They reported fewer negative physical symptoms such as headaches or colds. And they were active in many ways that were good for them. Those who were grateful quite simply enjoyed a higher quality of life.

Emmons was surprised. "This is not just something that makes people happy, like a positive-thinking/optimism kind of thing. A feeling of gratitude really gets people to do something, to become more prosocial, more compassionate." Such was not the case in either of the other two groups.[3]

Try This

If you've never kept a gratitude journal, give it a whirl for just three weeks. It's easy to do. Choose a blank notebook or journal, and every evening, write down everything you were grateful for that day. Be specific, and have concrete experiences in mind. Why not try doing this experiment as a family?

LEARNING THE SOCIAL GRACE OF GRATITUDE

Researchers have proven what most parents probably know instinctively: gratitude doesn't come naturally. In her book *The Gift of Thanks*, Margaret Visser cites a study in which researchers observed how parents teach their children to say hi, thanks, and good-bye. The children in the study spontaneously said hi 27 percent of the time, good-bye 25 percent of the time, and thanks 7 percent of the time. Parents had to prompt their children to say hi 28 percent of the time, good-bye 33 percent of the time, and thanks 51 percent of the time.

In conclusion, children had a much more difficult time learning to say thanks. Most children have to learn to say thank you even before they know what it means. Visser states, "Eventually, when [children] have matured and been further educated, they will come to be able to feel the emotion that the words express. The words come first, the feelings later."

Based on this research Visser concludes that learning to be thankful involves a steep learning curve. She writes,

"In our culture thanksgiving is believed to be, for most children, the very last of basic social graces they acquire."[4] But it doesn't have to be. If you cultivate the attitude of gratitude around your dinner table on a routine basis, your children will embody gratitude more readily and abundantly than you might expect.

DISCUSSION STARTERS

- How many times do you think you might have said thank you today?
- What one thing are you especially grateful for today?
- Who is the most grateful person you know and why?
- What do you appreciate most about your family this week?
- How do you feel when you do something nice for people and they forget to say thank you?
- Can you think of one time when you regretted not saying thank you?
- To whom would you most like to express appreciation right now?

TRY A "YOU ARE SPECIAL" PLATE!

Doug and Margo Engberg have four adopted children—Gave, Tycie, Jazzmyn, and Mia—and they determined to make family dinnertime a part of their routine. As a busy couple, both working full time, this wasn't easy. But they've found their groove, and their dinners are often a time to celebrate someone's accomplishment. It all started with a fancy red "You Are Special" plate they pull out and use only to honor a family member who has reached a milestone (lost a first tooth) or accomplished a great feat (scored well on an important math test). And on these occasions, the special dessert is most often cupcakes.

In fact, Margo's cupcakes became such a family hit that the kids thought Mom should open up her own cupcake store. And believe it or not, that's just what she and Doug did. They opened PinkaBella Cupcakes at a shopping center near their home in Kirkland, Washington, and they now have three PinkaBella shops around Seattle. These delectable little confections are so good they recently won the coveted "Best of Western Washington" award. (Guess who got the "You Are Special" plate at dinner that night!)

FINDING OUT WHAT OUR KIDS ARE GRATEFUL FOR

In one of his books, writer Robert Fulghum tells the story of when his daughter was a little girl and gave him a paper bag to take with him to work. When he asked what was in the bag, she answered, "Just some stuff. Take it with you."

When he sat at his desk for lunch the next day, he pulled out the paper bag and poured out its contents: two hair ribbons, three small stones, a plastic dinosaur, a pencil stub, a tiny seashell, two animal crackers, a marble, used lipstick, two chocolate kisses, a small doll, and thirteen pennies. He chuckled, finished his lunch, and swept everything off into the wastebasket.

When he arrived at home that evening, his daughter asked him where the bag was. He told her he had left it at the office and asked why.

"Well," she said, "those are my things in the sack, Daddy, the ones I really like. I thought you might like to play with them, but now I want them back."

When she saw him hesitate, tears welled up in her eyes. "You didn't lose the bag, did you, Daddy?"

He said he didn't and that he would bring it home the next day. After she went to bed, he raced back to the office. Fulghum writes, "Molly had given me her treasures. All that a seven-year-old held dear. Love in a paper sack. And I had missed it. Not only missed it but had thrown it away because 'there wasn't anything in there I needed.' . . . It wasn't the first or last time I felt my 'Daddy Permit' was about to run out. It was a long trip back to the office. But there was nothing else to be done. . . . Just ahead of the janitor, I picked up the wastebasket and poured the contents on my desk. I was sorting it all out when the janitor came in to do his chores.

"'Lose something?'

"'Yeah, my mind!'"

When Fulghum found the bag, he uncrumpled it and filled it again with his daughter's items. After dinner the next evening, he sat down with Molly and had her tell him the story of every treasure in the bag.[5]

Fulghum goes on to say that it took a very long time for Molly to talk about each treasure. But that's what finding out what makes our children tick, what they value, and what they hold dear is really all about—taking time with them. That's why family dinners are so important. They build time to talk with our kids.

A TRUE CELEBRATION

Our first son, John, was a preemie, weighing in at just a pound and a half at birth and measuring just twelve inches in length. This is the story of our first years with John:

A full-term baby is about five times heavier and more than half a foot longer. A mother can wrap her thumb and middle finger around the leg of her baby; I could place my hand on John's back and touch my fingertips at his bellybutton. John weighed only a little more than a Venti Frappuccino.

Preemies struggle to eat. To learn to suck, swallow, and breathe is a large task for such a small being. It was almost impossible for John, whose digestive system hadn't formed properly. . . . After two weeks, John had to undergo surgery.

> Tell God what you need, and thank him for all he has done.
>
> PHILIPPIANS 4:6

The surgery was successful. John slowly recovered. He was able to eat, and we slowly began to settle into a routine. . . . But John was never able to feed naturally. At first he used a tube and then tiny bottles that were smaller than the ones I had used with my baby dolls as a child. He drank two cc's at a time, every two hours. That's about a teaspoonful of milk.

Many chronic challenges followed. . . . Food was threatening, not pleasurable. The simple task of

eating, taking in nutrients, and nurturing his little
body became insurmountable. From the age of one,
John was working with a speech therapist on feeding
issues. More than a year passed with little progress. . . .

When we discovered a new, experimental
group program, we jumped at the opportunity to
participate. Every week we journeyed to Children's
Hospital and met with Lynn, our capable speech
therapist, and a small group of young children and
their moms who shared many of the same challenges
with food that Johnny had. . . .

The power of a peer influence was a great tool for
both the children and the parents. During the twelve
weeks of the group, John faced each session with
anxiety. It was challenging to his core. Eating was
downright scary for John. The demands placed on
him to eat were exceedingly hard for his little "pleaser"
personality to cope with. The therapist and the
treatment were excellent, but at the end of the course
Lynn handed out "graduation" certificates to all the
children except for John.

John received a gentle, carefully framed "invitation"
to come back for the next group. Which we did. And
the next one after that. . . .

Looking back, I can't identify when things began
to change. They just did. At five years of age, John
finally tasted, and swallowed, and digested, his first
bites of fruit and vegetables and meat. Until that time,
the only food he had mastered was cheese. Cheese
probably saved his life. . . .

John is still a picky eater. . . . Every time I see [him] take a bite of salmon, or spinach, or even lick an ice cream cone, I marvel. It's a miracle. . . .

Grace before a meal is less a ritual than a time of true celebration. "Give us this day our daily bread." And thank you, really, for the ability to eat it.[6]

FROM STEPHANIE

My friend Becki had three daughters who were busy with sports, dancing, and church activities. Evenings were the busiest times of the week, and dinner together simply couldn't be managed. The solution was to have breakfast together every morning. They all were at the table at six o'clock! At first the girls were not too cheery, but as the years went on, having breakfast together became the norm, and everyone looked forward to those early-morning times. The breakfast recipe on the next page can be made ahead of time and even freezes well. Having breakfast food at dinnertime can be fun too!

Tomato Bacon Egg Strata (serves 6 to 8)

4 cups of cubed sourdough bread with crust

½ cup minced sun-dried tomatoes

1 cup diced tomatoes

1 teaspoon dried basil

2 tablespoons dried parsley

1 teaspoon chopped garlic

1 teaspoon kosher salt

½ teaspoon pepper

½ cup cooked bacon crumbles

2 cups shredded Swiss or mozzarella cheese

1 cup nonfat liquid egg product

2 cups nonfat milk

Spray a 9 x 13 baking dish with nonstick cooking spray. Layer first 10 ingredients in the order given. Pour egg and milk over the top and cover. Refrigerate overnight or freeze to use later.

If you've frozen the dish, thaw completely. Preheat oven to 350°. Bake covered for 35 minutes; then remove cover and bake 30 to 45 minutes until golden brown. Let stand for 10 minutes before serving.

11 | Starting a Fix-and-Freeze Club

FROM STEPHANIE

When I was growing up, we came home from school, had a
snack, and took off to play with our neighborhood friends.
The rule was that when the streetlights came on it was time
to come home! We played hide-and-seek and hopscotch,
rode bikes, and made forts in our backyards. When we got
home, Mom had dinner ready, and all we had to do was
wash up and sometimes help set the table. How times have
changed! When my own children were growing up during
their school years, the last thing I would have let them do is
leave the house at three to run around, their whereabouts
unknown to me until six or seven in the evening! Unfortunately, we no longer live in the era when it was safe to do
that, but we still need to keep our kids busy after school.
So I did what my girlfriends did. I enrolled my children in
music lessons, sports activities, church groups, and play
dates. They kept active and busy, and I drove them to their

events. So when did I have time to cook dinner? Freezer dinners to the rescue!

Being able to pull dinners out of the freezer three times a week from food I had assembled in advance helped to keep me from driving through a fast-food place on the way home from an event. And the biggest advantage? I didn't have to spend those days thinking about what we were going to do for dinner!

■ ■ ■

There are lots of benefits to family dinners: better nutrition, more family time and conversation, and so on; we've talked about these throughout this book. But another benefit you may not have thought of to belonging to a fix-and-freeze club is the chance to spend an evening with your friends, enjoy laughter and conversation, and at the end of the evening, have a supply of homemade meals ready to go into the freezer! Naturally, we'd love to have you get involved in Dream Dinners, but if you don't have a Dream Dinners location close to you (check out www.DreamDinners.com to find locations), here are a few ideas you can use to create your own fix-and-freeze club with a group of friends.

GETTING STARTED

It's a good idea to partner with the same group of friends in the beginning. To be fair, assign one person to each of the tasks on the next page, and then rotate the assignments each month. The following are the monthly responsibilities:

- The *Host* of the assembly session.
- The *Organizer* of the dinners. Members of the group can contribute their favorite recipes, and the Organizer collates the shopping lists. (There is some really good software for cooking that can help with this task.)
- The *Big-Box Shopper*, who receives a buying list from the Organizer and obtains the items on her list.
- The *Grocery-Store Shopper*, who receives a buying list from the Organizer and shops for those items.
- The *Babysitter*, who cares for the children while moms are assembling dinners (the other moms assemble her dinners as well as their own).

SET A DATE

Set a date for assembling the dinners, and have the host for that session send reminders and follow up with the shopper to be sure everything will be in supply. You'll also want to set the time. It's best to allow four to seven hours, depending on how many dinners you are making. We recommend that each member of the group make twelve dinners (plus the babysitter's share) because three nights a week busy families are tempted to eat out or eat junk food, and having three nights' worth of dinners in the freezer will help to avoid giving in to that temptation.

> That's something I've noticed about food: whenever there's a crisis if you can get people to eating normally things get better.
> **MADELEINE L'ENGLE**

GET COOKING

Use large containers (I like to use bus tubs—containers often used in restaurants for clearing tables) for mixing the ingredients for each recipe. That way you can make all sauces, pastas, marinades, and so forth in big batches and then divide them equally among the dinners when assembling.

> The best inheritance a parent can give to his children is a few minutes of their time each day.
>
> M. GRUNDLER

Members can bring their own baking pans, or you can purchase foil pans. Just don't forget to spray the pans with a good nonstick cooking spray before adding ingredients. And if you want to remove the dinners from the baking pans after they are frozen so that your pans are not in the freezer and unavailable for use, line the baking pans with heavy-duty foil, assemble the dinners, cover with foil, and freeze. Then you can remove the frozen dinners from the pans and seal tightly with the foil before putting them back in the freezer.

TIPS FOR SUCCESS

Of course, as your group works together, you'll learn what is best for you in many areas. But the following are some tips to help get you started and enjoy success sooner rather than later:

- When preparing pasta dishes, cook the pasta just until it's slightly softened. That way it won't end up mushy after the dinner is assembled, frozen, thawed, and then cooked.
- Dice all your onions at once, then just use as needed in each recipe.
- Use dry herbs. They hydrate into the dinner as they are thawing and impart more flavor than fresh herbs that have been frozen.
- Cook a large batch of chicken breasts to chop or shred as needed. Bring a large pot of water to a boil, add the chicken, and simmer 5 to 10 minutes or until a meat thermometer reads 160°. Drain and set aside for use in multiple recipes.
- When using sealable freezer bags, remove as much air as possible before sealing tightly. Lay them flat so that you can stack them on top of one another, taking up less space in the freezer.
- Turn on some fun music while your group is cooking and assembling. It will keep everyone moving and maybe even singing together!

Before finishing, set a date for the next fix-and-freeze session, and choose the next Host, Organizer, Big-Box Shopper, Grocery-Store Shopper, and Babysitter.

Have you ever heard the illustration about the walnuts and the rocks? In Steven Covey's book *First Things First*, he shares a story he heard from one of his associates.

I attended a seminar once where the instructor was lecturing on time. At one point, he said, "Okay, it's time for a quiz." He reached under the table and pulled out a wide-mouthed gallon jar. He set it on a table next to a platter with some fist-sized rocks on it. "How many of these rocks do you think we can get in the jar?" he asked. After we made our guess, he said, "Okay. Let's find out. He set one rock in the jar . . . then another . . . then another. I don't remember how many he got in, but he got the jar full. Then he asked, "Is that jar full?"

Everyone looked at the rocks and said, "Yes."

Then he said, "Ahh." He reached under the table and pulled out a bucket of gravel. Then he dumped some gravel in and shook the jar and the gravel went in all the little spaces left by the big rocks. Then he grinned and said once more, "Is the jar full?"

By this time we were on to him. "Probably not," we said.

"Good!" he replied. And he reached under the table and brought out a bucket of sand. He started dumping the sand in and it went in all the little spaces left by the rocks and the gravel. Once more he looked at us and said, "Is the jar full?"

"No!" we all roared.

He said, "Good!" and he grabbed a pitcher of water and began to pour it in. He got something like a quart of water in that jar. Then he said, "Well, what's the point?"

Somebody said, "Well, there are gaps, and if

you really work at it, you can always fit more into your life."

"No," he said, "that's not the point. The point is this: if you hadn't put these big rocks in first, would you ever have gotten any of them in?"[1]

What are the big rocks in your life? A project that you want to complete? Time with your loved ones? Your faith, your education, or your finances? A cause? Teaching or mentoring others? Remember that these big rocks need to go in first, or you'll never get them in at all. The hour that matters most needs to be a big rock. It represents what you want for your family.

> # Action expresses priorities.
>
> CHARLES A. GARFIELD

FROM STEPHANIE
Salads were not usually my children's favorite dinner, but this one was! After all, who ever heard of baking a salad? When I made the recipe on the next page and served it, everyone had to laugh. "Mom baked a salad!"

Asian Chopped Chicken Salad (serves 6)

3 cups cooked and chopped chicken

2 cups chopped celery

½ cup sliced almonds

1 chopped green bell pepper

1 cup chopped green onions

1 cup sliced carrots

⅓ cup sliced water chestnuts

1 cup chopped baby corn

3 tablespoons lemon juice

1 teaspoon kosher salt

4 tablespoons light soy sauce

1 tablespoon sesame oil

1 cup low-fat sesame dressing

2 cups dry chow mein noodles

Preheat oven to 350º. Spray a 9 x 13 baking dish with nonstick cooking spray. Combine all ingredients except noodles and spread evenly in the baking dish. Top with noodles, and bake uncovered for 25 to 35 minutes.

Conclusion

The Good-Enough Family Meal

If a thing is worth doing, it is worth doing badly.

G. K. CHESTERTON

HAVE YOU EVER HEARD the wonderful story "Babette's Feast" by Isak Dinesen? It's about a strict, dour, fundamentalist community in Denmark. Babette works as a cook for two elderly sisters who have no idea that she once was a chef to nobility back in her native France. Babette's dream is to return to her beloved home city of Paris, so every year she buys a lottery ticket in hopes of winning enough money to return. And every night her austere employers demand that she cook the same dreary meal—boiled fish and potatoes—because, they say, Jesus commanded, "Take no thought of food and drink."

One day the unbelievable happens: Babette wins the lottery! The prize is ten thousand francs, a small fortune.

And because the anniversary of the founding of the community is approaching, Babette asks if she might prepare a French dinner for the entire village.

At first the townspeople refuse: "No, it would be sin to indulge in such rich food." Babette begs them, and finally they relent. But the people secretly vow not to enjoy the feast, believing God will not blame them for eating this sinful meal as long as they do not enjoy it.

Babette begins her preparations. Caravans of exotic food arrive in the village, along with cages of quail and barrels of fine wine.

Finally the big day comes, and the villagers gather. The first course is an exquisite turtle soup. While they usually eat in silence, a little conversation begins to emerge with each spoonful of soup consumed. The atmosphere changes. Someone smiles. Someone else giggles. An arm comes up and drapes over a shoulder. Someone is heard to say, "After all, did not the Lord Jesus say, 'Love one another'?" By the time the entrée of quail arrives, those austere, pleasure-fearing people are giggling and laughing and slurping and guffawing and praising God for their many years together.

This pack of pharisees is transformed into a loving community through the gift of a meal. One of the two sisters goes into the kitchen to thank Babette, saying, "Oh, how we will miss you when you return to Paris!" And Babette replies, "I will not be returning to Paris because I have no money. I spent it all on the feast."[1]

We want to leave you with this story to remind you that family dinners prepared by loving hands can be transformative. They have that kind of power. They soften hearts. They build connection. They engender laughter. They cultivate caring attitudes. The simple but intentional ritual of breaking bread together can do more for your family than anyone might ever imagine.

And here's the good news: you don't have to be perfect. You will succeed wildly even if you are merely "good enough."

YOU'RE DOING BETTER THAN YOU THINK

The late British psychiatrist D. W. Winnicott put forth the idea of "good-enough mothering." He was convinced that mothering could never be perfect because of the mother's own emotional needs. The same applies to fathers. "Good enough" refers to the imperfect, though adequate, provision of emotional care that can raise a healthy child.

This idea of being "good enough" is essential to keeping your attempts at a meaningful family dinner hour from getting waylaid by over-amped expectations and inclinations toward perfectionism. After all, you have expectations, right? We all do. When you work to put a meal on the table, you expect your family not only to eat what you serve but also to like it. You expect compliments and kindness. You hope to have engaging conversation, good manners, and lots of laughter. You want warm and tender connections between everyone around the table.

But hear this clearly: not every dinner hour is magical. Sometimes the meal doesn't turn out well. Sometimes the kids are cranky. Sometimes there's an emotional outburst.

THE HOUR THAT MATTERS MOST

Sometimes you'll wonder if family dinners are worth the effort.

That's okay. What you're doing is good enough.

The goodness that stems from the hour that matters most is not evident on a nightly basis. Rather, the effect is cumulative. It's found in the consistency of the routine. It's evident as the ritual takes root and grows over time. Memory-making moments will emerge. So don't be discouraged. *Your efforts matter more than you know!*

FROM STEPHANIE

Almost any leftover food can go into scrambled eggs for breakfast or dinner: leftover Mexican food, chopped up with some fresh mushroom slices and cheese. Leftover steak with some browned onions and fresh sliced tomatoes in eggs. Leftover salmon with capers, cream cheese, and dill. Easy and delicious! Here's an egg recipe we especially enjoy:

Spanish Eggs (serves 6)

3 cups nonfat liquid egg product
½ cup flour
1 teaspoon kosher salt
½ teaspoon pepper
½ cup diced mild green chilies
1 pint cottage cheese
1 cup shredded cheddar cheese
1 cup shredded Monterey Jack cheese
4 dashes of Tabasco sauce
4 ten-inch tortillas

Preheat oven to 400°. In a large mixing bowl whisk eggs, flour, salt, and pepper. Add chilies, Tabasco sauce, and cheeses, and blend together. Cut tortillas in half, and then slice into half-inch strips. Fold into egg-and-cheese mixture.

Spray a 9 x 13 baking dish with nonstick cooking spray. Pour egg mixture into pan, cover, and freeze if desired. When ready to serve, thaw and bake 35 to 45 minutes, until set. Then broil on high just until brown. Let stand for 5 minutes before serving.

Notes

INTRODUCTION: ONCE UPON A MEALTIME

1. Robert Putnam, *Bowling Alone: The Collapse and Revival of American Community* (New York: Simon & Schuster, 2000).

CHAPTER 1: CREATING THE SAFEST PLACE ON EARTH

1. Merriam-Webster's Collegiate Dictionary, 11th ed., s.v. "comfort."
2. Nick and Nancy Stinnett and Joe and Alice Beam, *Fantastic Families: Six Proven Steps to Building a Strong Family* (New York: Howard, 1999).

CHAPTER 2: THE FAMILY MEAL: WHY BOTHER?

1. Anne Carey and Veronica Salazar, "Most Popular Activities at Dinnertime," *USA Today*, April, 12, 2010, based on a 2009 survey by the NPD Group and Dinnertime MealScape.
2. Jaine Carter and James D. Carter, "Eating Together Strengthens Family Ties," Scripps Howard News Service, www.newschief.com/stories /022799/lif_family.shtml (site unavailable).
3. K. W. Cullen and T. Baranowski, "Influence of Family Dinner on Food Intake of 4th to 6th Grade Students" (paper presented at the American Dietetic Association's Food and Nutrition Conference, October 2000).
4. "Learning by Example: How Family Meal Times Could Make 'Good Eating' Easier to Swallow," www.ipsos-mori.com/researchpublications /researcharchive/1770/Learning-By-Example-How-Family-Meal-Times-Could-Make-Good-Eating-Easier-To-Swallow.aspx. Posted February 10, 1999.
5. K. D. Stanek, D. Abbott, and S. Cramer, "Diet Quality and the Eating Environment of Preschool Children," *Journal of the American Dietetic Association* 90, no. 11 (November 1990): 1582–84.
6. "Family Dinner Experiments," transcript from *The Oprah Winfrey Show*, November 19, 1993.
7. *The Importance of Family Dinners VI*, The National Center on Addiction and Substance Abuse at Columbia University, September 2010.
8. *The Importance of Family Dinners VI*.
9. "What Makes America's Youth Happy?" Knowledge Networks Inc. (April 2007).
10. Nancy Gibbs, "The Magic of the Family Meal," *Time*, June 12, 2006, 51–56.
11. Jenet Jacob, "Work, Family, and Individual Factors Associated with

Mothers Attaining Their Preferred Work Situations," *Family & Consumer Sciences Research Journal* 36, no. 3 (July 2009): 208–228.

CHAPTER 3: RECOVERING THE LOST ART OF EATING TOGETHER

1. Molly Logan Anderson, "Sit-Down Dinner: Rediscover the Lost Art of the Family Meal," April 20, 2010, www.galesburg.com/lifestyles /x749207802/Sit-down-dinner-Rediscover-the-lost-art-of-the-family-meal.
2. "Learning by Example: How Family Meal Times Could Make 'Good Eating' Easier to Swallow," www.ipsos-mori.com/researchpublications /researcharchive/1770/Learning-By-Example-How-Family-Meal-Times-Could-Make-Good-Eating-Easier-To-Swallow.aspx. Posted February 10, 1999.
3. www.focusonthefamily.com/entertainment/mediawise/tv-and-todays-family/is-america-addicted-to-television.aspx.

CHAPTER 4: THE HEART OF GREAT TABLE TALK

1. Adapted from Les and Leslie Parrott, *The Parent You Want to Be: Who You Are Matters More Than What You Do* (Grand Rapids: Zondervan, 2007), 65–66.
2. Adapted from Les and Leslie Parrott, *Trading Places* (Grand Rapids: Zondervan, 2008), 23–25.
3. Adapted from Parrott, *Trading Places*, 27.
4. L. Newton, "Overconfidence in the Communication of Intent: Heard and Unheard Melodies," PhD diss., Stanford University, 1990.
5. Parrott, *Trading Places*, 39–41.
6. Parrott, *Trading Places*, 83.
7. John C. Maxwell, *Winning with People* (Nashville: Nelson, 2004), 73.

CHAPTER 5: HOW TO LISTEN SO YOUR KIDS TALK

1. Adapted from Les and Leslie Parrott, *The Parent You Want to Be* (Grand Rapids, Zondervan, 2007), 96.
2. Adapted from Les Parrott, *Helping the Struggling Adolescent* (Grand Rapids: Zondervan, 2000), 35.
3. Adapted from Parrott, *Helping the Struggling Adolescent*, 35.
4. Adapted from Les and Leslie Parrott, *The Parent You Want to Be*, 89.
5. Adapted from Parrott, *The Parent You Want to Be*, 94–95.
6. Adapted from Les and Leslie Parrott, *Love Talk* (Grand Rapids: Zondervan, 2004), 132.
7. Charles R. Swindoll, *Man to Man* (Grand Rapids: Zondervan, 1996), 272.

CHAPTER 6: CURBING CONFLICT AT THE TABLE AND BEYOND

1. Adapted from Les and Leslie Parrott, *The Parent You Want to Be* (Grand Rapids, Zondervan, 2007), 146–47.
2. John Gottman, PhD, "Effects on Marriage of a Psycho-Communicative-Educational Intervention with Couples Undergoing the Transition to Parenthood," *Journal of Family Communication* 5 (2005): 1–24.
3. George Lewis, "Are Ya Kidding Me?! No Complaints for 21 Days," http://today.msnbc.msn.com/id/17362505, accessed April 2, 2011.
4. Les and Leslie Parrott, *Saving Your Marriage before It Starts* (Grand Rapids: Zondervan, 1995), 131–32.

CHAPTER 7: ENJOYING MORE LAUGHTER

1. Martin Grotjahn, *Beyond Laughter: Humor and the Subconscious* (New York: McGraw, 1957).
2. Les Parrott and Leslie L. Parrott, *The Love List: Eight Little Things That Make a Big Difference in Your Marriage* (Grand Rapids: Zondervan, 2002), 35.
3. Parrott, *The Love List*, 42–43.
4. Parrott, *The Love List*, 42–43.

CHAPTER 8: CULTIVATING DEEPER VALUES

1. Opening paragraphs have been adapted from Les and Leslie Parrott, *The Parent You Want to Be* (Grand Rapids: Zondervan, 2007), 25–26.
2. C. Heath and D. Heath, *Made to Stick* (New York: Random House, 2007). See page 119 for how this exercise and principle apply to communicating any idea.
3. Adapted from Les and Leslie Parrott, *The Love List: Eight Little Things That Make a Big Difference in Your Marriage* (Grand Rapids: Zondervan, 2002), 61–63.
4. Quoted in Parrott, *The Love List*, 64.
5. Karen Springen, "Raising a Moral Child," special issue, *Newsweek* (Fall/Winter 2000): 71.
6. Po Bronson, "Learning to Lie," *New York* magazine, February 10, 2008.
7. Dan Millman, "Sachi," in Jack Canfield and Mark Victor Hansen, *Chicken Soup for the Soul: 101 Stories to Open the Heart and Rekindle the Spirit* (Deerfield Beach, FL: Health Communications, 1993), 290.
8. "Parents Do Little about Kids' Faith Training," *Southeast Outlook*, May 22, 2003.
9. "Theo's Economic Lesson," *The Cosby Show*, season 1, episode 1, written by Michael Lesson, Ed Weinberger, and Bill Cosby, aired September 20, 1984 (Urban Works, 2005), DVD.

10. Mary Story, PhD, RD, and Dianne Neumark-Sztainer, PhD, MPH, RD, "A Perspective on Family Meals: Do They Matter?" *Nutrition Today* 40, no. 6 (November/December 2005): 261–266. See also http://journals .lww.com/nutritiontodayonline/Fulltext/2005/11000/A_Perspective _on_Family_Meals_Do_They_Matter_.7.aspx?WT.mc _id=HPxADx20100319xMP#P54. Accessed March 24, 2010.

11. J. Strayer and W. Roberts, "Empathy and Observed Anger and Aggression in Five-Year-Olds," *Social Development* 13 (2004): 11.

12. Adapted from Les and Leslie Parrott, *The Parent You Want to Be*, 113–14.

13. Adapted from Leslie Parrott, *The First Drop of Rain* (Grand Rapids: Zondervan, 2009), 45–46.

14. "*Cloudy with a Chance of Meatballs*: A Father's Struggle to Communicate with His Son," www.preachingtoday.com/illustrations /2010/june/3061410.html.

15. Bronson, "Learning to Lie."

16. Nancy Darling, quoted in Po Bronson, "Learning to Lie." See also http://nymag.com/news/features/43893. Accessed April 11, 2011.

CHAPTER 9: INSTILLING GENTLE MANNERS

1. *Pygmalion* (Pascal Film Productions, 1938), written by George Bernard Shaw, directed by Anthony Asquith and Leslie Howard. In 1964, Warner Bros. released the classic musical *My Fair Lady*, which is another version of the same story.

2. George Bernard Shaw, *Pygmalion* (Stilwell, KS: Digireads.com Publishing, 2005), 67–72.

3. John Gottman, PhD, "Effects on Marriage of a Psycho-Communicative-Educational Intervention with Couples Undergoing the Transition to Parenthood," *Journal of Family Communication* 5 (2005): 1–24.

4. John Gottman, PhD, *Raising an Emotionally Intelligent Child: The Heart of Parenting* (New York: Simon & Schuster, 1997), 25.

5. Judith Warner, "Kids Gone Wild," *New York Times*, November 27, 2005.

6. Warner, "Kids Gone Wild."

7. This anecdote or a similar one has appeared in multiple sources, including Edward K. Rowell and Bonne L. Steffen, *Humor for Preaching and Teaching from Leadership Journal & Christian Reader* (Grand Rapids: Baker, 1998). In this occurrence, the author has personalized some of the details.

8. Charles Swindoll, "Laugh Again," *Christianity Today* 39, no. 3.

9. Mary Mitchell and John Corr, *The Complete Idiot's Guide to Etiquette* (New York: Penguin, 2000), 12.

10. Adapted from Les and Leslie Parrott, *Your Time-Starved Marriage* (Grand Rapids: Zondervan, 2006), 102.

11. Carl Honoré, *In Praise of Slowness: How a Worldwide Movement Is Challenging the Cult of Speed* (New York: HarperCollins, 2004), 59.

CHAPTER 10: COUNTING YOUR BLESSINGS

1. Adapted from Les and Leslie Parrott, *Your Time-Starved Marriage* (Grand Rapids: Zondervan, 2006), 103.

2. Steve Moore, "A Graceful Goodbye," *Leadership* (Summer 2002), 41–42. The Jewish poet and storyteller Noah ben Shea tells a parable.

3. "Gratitude Is Good for Your Health," www.preachingtoday.com /illustrations/2007/november/5112607.html, accessed April 11, 2011. See also Deborah Norville, "How the New Science of Thank-You Can Change Your Life," *Reader's Digest*, October 2007.

4. Margaret Visser, *The Gift of Thanks* (New York: Houghton Mifflin Harcourt, 2009), 8–15.

5. Adapted from Robert Fulghum, *It Was on Fire When I Lay Down on It* (New York: Ivy Books, 1991), 26–29.

6. Leslie Parrott, *The First Drop of Rain* (Grand Rapids: Zondervan, 2009), 79–82.

CHAPTER 11: STARTING A FIX-AND-FREEZE CLUB

1. Steven Covey, *First Things First* (New York: Fireside, 1995), 88–89.

CONCLUSION: THE GOOD-ENOUGH FAMILY MEAL

1. This summary is taken from Les and Leslie Parrott, *Your Time-Starved Marriage* (Grand Rapids: Zondervan, 2006), 105–106. See also Isak Dinesen, *Babette's Feast and Other Anecdotes of Destiny* (New York: Vintage, 1988).

About the Authors

LES AND LESLIE PARROTT, PHDS, are codirectors of the Center for Relationship Development on the campus of Seattle Pacific University and the bestselling authors of the award-winning book *Saving Your Marriage before It Starts*. They have also written *Love Talk, Trading Places, The Parent You Want to Be, High-Maintenance Relationships* (Les), and with John C. Maxwell, *25 Ways to Win with People* (Les). The Parrotts are sought-after speakers and hold an average of forty relationship seminars across North America annually. They have been featured in *USA Today*, the *Wall Street Journal*, and the *New York Times*. Their many television appearances include *The View, The O'Reilly Factor, CNN, Good Morning America*, and *Oprah*. Les and Leslie live in Seattle with their two sons. To learn more, visit their website at www.RealRelationships.com.

STEPHANIE ALLEN is a recognized pioneer in the meal-assembly industry. She brings an extensive background in the food industry, including eighteen years of recipe development and catering. Stephanie first began making fix-and-freeze meals for her own family in 1986 and gradually began developing a collection of specialized "dream dinners" recipes. She soon became deluged with requests to expand her time-saving meal assembly solutions with others. When the demand became overwhelming, she enlisted the help of longtime friend and experienced business manager Tina Kuna, and in 2002, they hosted the first series of large-scale meal assembly sessions, which became the catalyst for opening the first Dream Dinners store.

A popular speaker and educator, Stephanie spreads her vision to make people's lives easier and restore the tradition of family dinners.

TINA KUNA, a recognized innovative leader in the meal-assembly industry, was instrumental in creating the groundbreaking Dream Dinners business model, which has become the industry standard.

A working mother of three, Kuna adopted the assemble-and-freeze method for her family in 1996, taught by eventual business partner Stephanie Allen. A strong advocate of families eating together, Tina plays a key role in bringing the Dream Dinners solution to communities across the nation.

In 2006, Tina and Stephanie received the Ernst and Young Entrepreneur Of The Year award in the Pacific Northwest.

ALSO FROM LES PARROTT, PH.D.

✦ ✦ ✦

The Control Freak
Need help coping with control freaks or identifying your own controlling tendencies? Self-tests will help you find out whether you are suffering from a controlling relationship—or how controlling you can be. They'll also help provide a lifelong prescription for healthier relationships. Learn how to relate with a coercive or supervising person, how to relinquish unhealthy control, and how to repair relationships damaged by overcontrol.
978-0-8423-3793-9 Softcover

High-Maintenance Relationships
How do you handle a friend who saps your energy? When do you love without limit? We've all asked these questions. And too often our responses are either to back out of relationships or to give up on impossible people. Dr. Les Parrott shows us other options, including setting boundaries, giving the gift of grace, and leaving room for God. This book will give you practical tools by devoting chapters to the Martyr, The Cold Shoulder, The Critic, the Volcano, The Gossip ... fifteen high maintenance relationships in all.
978-0-8423-1466-4 Softcover

The One Year Love Talk Devotional for Couples
Offering wisdom and insights for applying biblical truths to our relationships, this book encourages couples to connect and communicate every day. This practical, uplifting guide is perfect for busy couples who long to experience a stronger relationship and better communication. Easy-to-follow daily readings focus on loving each other the way God loves us.
978-1-4143-3739-5 Softcover

CP0112

SMALL GROUP *INSIGHTS*

Where Real Relationships Start

Successful small group experiences depend on authentic relationships. The better the connections, the better the group. And that's just what this tool will do for you.

- Simple
- Personalized
- Engaging
- Quick

Whatever your group's purpose, the Small Group Insights Profile provides you with a fast-track to authenticity and meaningful connection.

www.smallgroupinsights.com